GREAT
HOUSES OF
SCOTLAND

GREAT HOUSES OF
SCOTLAND

HUGH MONTGOMERY-MASSINGBERD
CHRISTOPHER SIMON SYKES

RIZZOLI
NEW YORK

For Ripples and Isabella

Note on public opening arrangements

By no means are all the houses featured in this book open to the public on a regular season-long basis. Some, such as Kinross, are only open by written appointment; others, such as Newhailes (currently under restoration), Yester and Ardkinglas are not, in the normal course of events, open at all. Several are only open for a limited period in the summer. In every case the reader is well advised to consult the standard annual guides (*Hudson's Historic Houses and Gardens* and Reed Information Services' *Historic Houses, Castles and Gardens*) for precise details and information as to dates, times, prices of admission, facilities, telephone numbers etc.

ENDPAPERS Plasterwork by Thomas Clayton in the entrance hall at Newhailes.

HALF-TITLE Leonine look-out on the roof at Gosford House, East Lothian.

FRONTISPIECE Ardkinglas on Loch Fyne.

First published in the United States of America in 1997 by
RIZZOLI INTERNATIONAL PUBLICATIONS, INC.
300 Park Avenue South, New York, NY 10010

First published in Great Britain in 1997 by
Laurence King Publishing

Text copyright © 1997 Hugh Montgomery-Massingberd
Photographs copyright © 1997 Christopher Simon Sykes

ISBN 0-8478-2038-6
LC 97-66472

Designed and typeset by Karen Stafford
Edited by Alison Wormleighton
Printed and bound by C.S. Graphics, Singapore

CONTENTS

INTRODUCTION

*I*N THE Sassenach comedian Tony Hancock's celebrated television sketch *The Blood Donor*, the curmudgeon of East Cheam, on ascertaining that the doctor is a Scot, proceeds to address him in the manner of Sir Harry Lauder – with a 'Hoots Mon', allusions to 'bricht moonlicht nichts' and other Caledonian clichés. 'We're not,' responds Patrick Cargill, as the medic, in his best Sandhurst drawl, '*all* Rob Roys'.

Similarly, most popular illustrated books on the subject of Scottish Heritage tend to be tartaned tributes to the hoary traditions of hackneyed picture-postcard Castles. Well-worn paths are trodden around bleak fortresses bedecked with sentimental legends. Somehow Scotland's no less splendid set of Great Houses has not received the attention it deserves. Perhaps this personal selection of fine family seats may open a few eyes unfamiliar with this much underrated dimension of Scottish social history?

Naturally, as a glance at the contents page will confirm, many (indeed almost a third) of the 26 houses featured in the book happen to rejoice in the name of 'Castle', that wide-ranging and much misunderstood term. Nor, we trust, does this eclectic collection of places lack for romance or colour – or blood, for that matter. Yet, on the whole, we have chosen to chronicle domestic, as opposed to defensive, building in its grandest forms.

The great houses that follow – in a loose chronological sequence based rather more on the length of tenure enjoyed on the estate by the family concerned than on the predominant architectural style of the present building – reflect the evolution and development of Scottish architecture through the centuries. The early, pre-1500, castles tended, for obvious defensive reasons, to concentrate their accommodation in a massive single tower, adjoined by a walled courtyard. Cawdor is a particularly good example of these 'compound' Scots houses, but such old towers still form the basis of several other structures where they are obscured by subsequent building work, as at Dunrobin.

PRECEDING PAGES The fairytale skyline above the sea shore at Dunrobin Castle, Sutherland.

LEFT Late 17th-century plasterwork ceiling at Thirlestane Castle, Berwickshire.

Indeed the tower long remained the principal 'type' for every scale of domestic building in Scotland. The typical tower-house of the 16th and 17th centuries was 'L'-shaped, with a staircase turret set in the internal angle. Glamis is the most striking specimen of this style, while the delightfully straightforward Traquair departs from the 'angular' arrangement.

The 'Auld Alliance' with France helped introduce Renaissance flourishes to Scotland from the 16th century onwards. Early 17th-century Scottish country houses may have resembled fortified castles – tall and narrow, with thick walls and small rooms – though their design was no longer inspired by considerations of defence alone, but also by a romantic medievalism. This was the same dream of chivalry which in the France of François I had produced the *châteaux* of the Loire.

With the accession of King James VI of Scotland to the English throne in 1603, though, the Scots nobles began to form part of the British Aristocracy instead of being, as had previously been the case, the aristocracy of another country – whether the French-orientated Lowland aristocracy in the reigns of King James V and Mary Queen of Scots or the old Gaelic-speaking tribal aristocracy of the Highlands. Now Scots aristocrats who hoped for advancement hurried south to the Jacobean Court. New ideas and fashions, emanating from the Low Countries and Italy, as well as England, were picked up.

Later in the 17th century, following the bitter aftermath of the Civil War, came the full flowering of the Scots Renaissance with such spectacular Baroque palaces as Drumlanrig. The architect of the lavish late-Stuart remodelling of Thirlestane, Sir William Bruce, went on to build Scotland's first purely Classical country houses such as Kinross and the original Hopetoun.

Notwithstanding the Act of Union with England in 1707, and the upheavals of the Jacobite Risings of 1715 and 1745, Classical architecture flourished amid the 18th-century Scottish Enlightenment. William Adam, the leading Scottish architect of the first half of the century, whose achievements have been unfairly overshadowed by the brilliance of his son Robert, designed a remarkably diverse range of country houses.

By way of redressing the balance, Adam senior's prolific output is very generously represented in this selection. Indeed, though not beyond criticism for his tampering with earlier work, William Adam is effectively the star of the show. His hand seems to be everywhere – Hopetoun, Yester, Mellerstain, Arniston, the House of Dun, Haddo, Duff, even Inveraray.

If William Adam has been hitherto underrated outside Scotland, so, paradoxically, Robert Adam – who went South and dominated the English architectural scene – has not perhaps received the recognition he deserves in his native land. He was, after all, responsible for the exquisite interiors at Mellerstain and the romantic cliff-top 'castle' of Culzean.

This harking back to the castle style in the late-18th century indicated the Scots' deep-seated yearning for the old traditions. It was soon to be fuelled by the stirring romances of Sir Walter Scott, Laird of Abbotsford, who helped heal the wounds of Culloden by masterminding King George IV's emotional visit to Scotland in 1822. Scott was the precursor of the Baronial Revival, a style which was somewhat over-developed later in the 19th century, principally by David Bryce, who remodelled Blair.

The 'discovery' of the Highlands, which had started with the Romantic Movement and Scott's novels, was furthered by the British aristocracy's love of sport and also by the coming of the railways. With Queen Victoria's purchase of Balmoral in 1848 the Highlands were really in vogue. A surging sea of tartan threatened to engulf Caledonia.

Later in the 19th century, the amazing High Victorian Gothic of Mount Stuart was rather in a category of its own. The story of the great house in Scotland, though, continues into the 20th century with the no less astonishing Edwardian opulence of Manderston, which adopted the 'Adam' style. Finally, we come full circle at the romantic shooting lodge of Ardkinglas, where Sir Robert Lorimer, the 'Scots Lutyens', sympathetically combined 17th-century vernacular with modern comfort.

It need hardly be said that the original photography laid out here captures the spirit and style of the houses infinitely better than words ever could.

Drawing Room, with Grinling Gibbons carvings, at Drumlanrig Castle.

Therefore the text is essentially as much about the landed dynasties who created these glorious temples of the arts as about the architecture and decoration.

By their very definition, great houses are the seats of great families. Accordingly, the great families of Scotland figure prominently in the narrative. The Royal House of Stuart is represented by such branches as the Maxwell Stuarts of Traquair and the Crichton-Stuarts, Marquesses of Bute, at Mount Stuart. The illustrious House of Hamilton, in the regrettable absence of the ducal Hamilton Palace (demolished in the 1920s), is represented by the Baillie-Hamiltons, Earls of Haddington, at Mellerstain. The Duke of Buccleuch, at Drumlanrig and Bowhill, flies the flag for Douglas and Scott respectively.

Ensuring that the Lowlands do not hog the limelight, the Clan Campbell fields its Chief, the Duke of Argyll, at Inveraray, and Earl Cawdor at Cawdor. The Murrays are represented by the Dukes of Atholl at Blair and the Earl of Mansfield at Scone.

Several Scots family fortunes were founded in the Law. The Dalrymples of Newhailes and the Dundases of Arniston are cases in point.

While retailing the family histories, and not neglecting the anecdotes that form part of aristocratic folklore, an attempt has been made to bring the story right up to date. Thus it is possible to celebrate the National Trust for Scotland's

Mount Stuart, Isle of Bute: detail of a turreted downpipe.

Gothic swimming pool at Mount Stuart.

ABOVE Entrance front of Yester House, East Lothian, from the bridge across Gifford Water.

BELOW 'Downstairs' bells at Ardkinglas, Argyll.

current rescue mission at Newhailes and its recent restorations of the House of Dun and Culzean. Enterprising new charitable trust schemes have brought new purpose and vigour to such palaces as Thirlestane, Hopetoun and Mount Stuart (magnificently restored by the late Marquess of Bute before his premature death in 1993). An initiative by the National Galleries of Scotland helped find an 'outstation' solution for the 'forgotten' splendours of Duff House. The Galleries' director, Tim Clifford, is one of the residents in Kit Martin's inspiring recent conversion of Tyninghame for multiple occupation – wherein the future of 'problem' great houses may well lie.

Far from the doom-gloom one so often encounters in the private sector of the Heritage world, the Scots joint is jumping. Everywhere you look there are encouraging signs that the present generation of private owners is taking a much more positive approach to great houses than their often unduly pessimistic, not to say philistine, predecessors. Such dedicated châtelaines as Althea Dundas Bekker (who is restoring the formerly dry-rot-ridden Arniston) and the Countess of Rosebery (who has stylishly rationalized the display of the collections at Dalmeny) communicate enthusiasm for the future. Gian Carlo Menotti plans an opera school at the beautifully redecorated Yester. The Duke of Buccleuch has won deserved acclaim as a champion of public-spirited land management and countryside education at Drumlanrig and Bowhill.

Up on Loch Fyne, the Duke of Argyll has rejuvenated Inveraray after a seemingly disastrous fire and John Noble's seafood business has revitalized Ardkinglas. Down on the Tweed strong ales are being brewed once more at Traquair. Happily, for the great houses of Scotland in general, there appears to be plenty of good stuff left in the bottle for future generations to savour.

1

BLAIR CASTLE

PERTHSHIRE

BLAIR – a palimpsest of Scottish history and architectural taste, turning first one way and then the other – illustrates the folly of seeking to impose a rigorous classification between Castles and Great Houses. At first glimpse from the new, greatly improved, 'high road' that runs from Perth to Inverness (the A9), the exciting elevated prospect shows us a massive white-harled facade, complete with crow-stepped gables and bartizans. Cradled by rugged, forest-clad mountains and surrounded by romantic rivers at the entrance to the Highland fastnesses of Glen Garry, this, one thinks, must be the ultimate Scotch Baronial pile, awash with clan history and tartan legend.

Yet, on closer inspection, the immediate setting of this seat of the Murrays, Dukes of Atholl, notwithstanding the mountains and the position some three miles above the fearsome Pass of Killiecrankie, exudes the controlled grandeur of aristocratic aestheticism. As we approach the castle we notice the hallmarks of a great house in its parkland element of tamed nature: an avenue of limes, verdant swards bedecked with confidently planted trees and terraces surveying the ducal domain.

Although the castellations outside and the armoury-encrusted entrance hall within do indeed turn out to be the work of the 'Baronial' architect David Bryce, dating from 1869, the interior springs a considerable surprise. For underneath the oh-so-Scottish skin is to be found a sumptuous temple of the Georgian arts richly adorned with Rococo plasterwork by Thomas Clayton (who worked with William Adam at the Royal Palace of Holyroodhouse in Edinburgh) and marble chimneypieces by Thomas Carter (a favourite craftsman of the Prince Regent). Here, then, is a Highland Castle which, as Mark Girouard has pointed out, became 'a treasure-house of mid-18th century English furniture and decoration'.

Yet it would be quite wrong to infer that there is something 'fake' about Blair as the tourist buses pull up in front of the kilted Castle Piper blowing away

PRECEDING PAGES The view from the 'high road': Blair Castle and the village of Blair Atholl set in the wide Strath of Garry.

LEFT The Georgian Front Staircase. The portrait of *James Moray (younger) of Abercairny* must have been painted after the 1745 Jacobite Rising, when the kilt was proscribed – which may explain why the picture was not signed (it is thought to be by Davison).

RIGHT The Entrance Hall, built in 1872 for the 7th Duke of Atholl by David and John Bryce. The display of arms includes rifles, targes, swords, crossbows and powder-horns.

manfully or the Atholl Highlanders (Britain's only surviving 'private army', a ceremonial bodyguard championed by Queen Victoria in an excess of Highland enthusiasm) parading to the strains of the Pipe Band. For, to borrow a Hollywood witticism about Ernest Hemingway to the effect that his chest wig disguised a genuinely hairy chest underneath, Blair, too, boasts authentic battlements behind the phoney turrets.

As befits a castle in such an obviously strategic situation, Blair was first fortified as far back as the 13th century. The Earldom of Atholl was one of the seven original Mormaerships of Scotland, the rulers of which were styled Mormaers in the 10th century and by early in the 12th century were known as Earls. These feudal chieftains commanded loyalty from thousands of Gaelic-speaking clansmen, a tradition that continued as the Earls of Atholl eventually became transmogrified into Marquesses and Dukes.

In the 13th century the Royal Celtic line of the original Earls of Atholl died out. The earldom passed to the Strathbogie dynasty, of whom David, the 'Crusader Earl', complained in 1269 to King Alexander III that, during his absence in England, John Comyn, or Cumming, of Badenoch had made an incursion into Atholl and begun building a castle at Blair. To this day the main tower of the castle is, by tradition, known as Cumming's Tower. A wing and a second tower were later to be added, also in the traditional Scottish castle style.

The Earldom of Atholl and Blair itself suffered many vicissitudes brought about by the buffetings of Anglo–Scottish history and the ever-conflicting loyalties demanded by the two Crowns. Thus, though the Crusader Earl's son and successor was a staunch supporter of King Robert Bruce, and ended up with his head fixed on London Bridge for his pains, subsequently the earldom was forfeited for opposition to Bruce. And so it passed like a shuttlecock until eventually, in 1457, the title was finally conferred upon King James II's maternal half-brother, Sir John Stewart of Balvenie, ancestor of the present Atholl family.

LEFT The Dining Room, originally a 16th-century banqueting hall, was transformed in the 18th century with magnificent plasterwork by Thomas Clayton (whose overmantel is filled with an exuberant trophy of arms) and Thomas Bardwell (whose ceiling features roundels of the Seasons). The wall panels, showing scenes of the local mountains, were painted by Charles Stewart, an early Scots landscape artist patronized by the 3rd Duke of Atholl.

BELOW Detail of Classical figure reclining on a pediment above one of Clayton's elaborately stuccoed doorcases in the Dining Room.

Like the history of the family, that of the castle has been nothing if not eventful. Frequently besieged, Blair has four times been occupied by opposing forces and partly destroyed, as well as being turned from a castle into a house and back into a castle again. King Edward III of England came to stay here in 1336; and a couple of centuries later Mary Queen of Scots was entertained to a great drive of 2,000 red deer. The bag of the hunt was 360 deer and five wolves.

By the time of Mary's visit considerable changes had taken place to the medieval castle, with the building extending southwards from Cumming's Tower. The Great Hall range, which connected the two towers, was built in about 1530 by the 3rd Earl of Atholl, who was celebrated for his magnificent hospitality. His son, the 4th Earl, Mary's host, is supposed to have been poisoned, whereas the 4th Earl's Countess was thought to possess powers of incantation.

During the Civil War John Murray, Master of Tullibardine, who acquired the Earldom of Atholl through his mother, heiress of the 5th Earl of the Stewart line, was an ardent Royalist and raised 1,800 men to support King Charles I. The dashing Cavalier Marquess of Montrose hoisted his standard at Blair in 1644. But eventually, eight years later, the castle was captured and held by Cromwell's troops until the Restoration of King Charles II.

The Athollmen who had rallied behind Montrose in 1644, however, were not to be found at the nearby Battle of Killiecrankie in 1689 when 'Bonnie' Dundee made his last stand for King James against the Dutch usurper, William of Orange. The reason was that the 1st Marquess of Atholl – whose wife, Lady Amelia Stanley, happened to be a cousin of 'King Billy' – played, to quote *The Complete Peerage*, 'a trimming and shuffling part' in the so-called 'Glorious Revolution'. Macaulay went further, describing the Marquess as 'the falsest, the most fickle, the most pusillanimous of mankind'.

LEFT The Picture Staircase, created in 1756 and redecorated in the 19th century, when the plaster and woodwork were grained. The full-length portrait is of the 1st Marquess of Atholl, painted by Jacob De Witt, or de Wet, in the late-17th-century Classical manner as Julius Caesar, with the Battle of Bothwell Brig proceeding vigorously under his baton.

BELOW The majestic Drawing Room, hung in crimson damask, with its coved ceiling rich in plasterwork by Thomas Clayton, who also carved the white marble chimneypiece. The picture above it is Johann Zoffany's bucolic conversation piece of the 3rd Duke of Atholl and his family. The pier glass mirrors were made by George Cole.

And so, in the nature of these things, the 2nd Marquess of Atholl – who, in fairness, initially opposed the Act of Union with England until he had obtained better terms for Scotland – duly became the 1st Duke of Atholl. Nonetheless, three of his sons came out in favour of the Jacobite cause in the abortive 1715 Rising. The divided loyalties of the Murrays were even more notable in the '45 when first Bonnie Prince Charlie stayed at Blair and then Lord George Murray, at the head of his Jacobite 'Atholl Brigade', went so far as to lay siege to the family seat, which was then occupied by Hanoverian troops. In the process, Blair gained the distinction of being the last castle in the British Isles to be besieged.

The Government-supporting 2nd Duke of Atholl – who had already embarked on an ambitious building and landscaping scheme before this belli-cose interruption – was not actually inside Blair when his brother, Lord George, was bombarding the place. Once peace was resumed, this Whig grandee was able to concentrate on a dozen years of remarkable architectural achievement, which were to witness the transformation of Blair from an antiquated castle to a modern country house set in an English-style park.

With the help of the architect James Winter, the old turrets and gables were removed, sash windows were installed, marble chimneypieces and new furniture shipped up from London (and carted by horse overland from Perth). Even the staircase, constructed in London by a carpenter called Abraham Swan, or Swain, was transported in sections to the Highlands.

This splendidly robust Picture Staircase (grained in the 19th century) rises dramatically through three storeys. At the top, under the castle roof, is the majestic Drawing Room, hung with crimson damask and boasting a coved and richly plastered ceiling. On the floor below, the delicious Green and White Dining Room is decorated with the most gloriously exuberant of Clayton's plasterwork: luxuriant swags of fruit above broken door-pediments and a riot of arms and armour over the chimneypiece. There is more flamboyant spectacle in the Tapestry Room (so-called for its Brussels tapestries that were made for King Charles I), which is dominated by a stupendous late 17th-century state bed complete with a canopy crowned by four outrageous tufts of ostrich feathers.

Altogether more than 30 rooms, culminating in the vast 1877 Ballroom, can be seen on the public tour at Blair and it would take the entire length of this book to do anything like justice to the treats on show. Not for nothing has Blair Castle been nicknamed 'the Highland Victoria & Albert'. The range of furniture, from early oak to Regency cabinets, is certainly of museum standard and the many fine portraits include two delightful conversation pieces of the 3rd and 4th Dukes of Atholl and their families by Johann Zoffany and David Allan respectively. The contrast in *genres* is particularly instructive: the 3rd Duke (*floruit* 1764–74) is portrayed as the consummate Whig swell, the 4th Duke (1774–1830) as every inch the Highland sportsman, bonneted and with a dead stag at his feet.

The Highland Revival found its full expression at Blair in the time of the 7th Duke of Atholl, who brought in Bryce to make it a castle once more. The two main towers were built up and capped with battlements and 'pepper-pot' turrets, another tower was added to form the new entrance and turreted wings were run out to the north and south. Fortunately, though, the 18th-century interior remained untouched.

Something of the feudal flavour of Blair was captured in the writings of Scotland's most colourful herald and historian, the late Sir Iain Moncreiffe of that Ilk, Bt, himself a kinsman of the Atholls. As a boy of 15, Moncreiffe witnessed the last great deer drive at Blair Atholl in 1934 when, as he recalled (shades of Mary Queen of Scots), 'over 900 beasts covered one side of Glentilt with their movement of massed reddish-brown for an incredible moment'. Staying with 'Cousin Bardie' (the Marquess of Tullibardine, later the 8th Duke of Atholl, who raised and commanded the Scottish Horse in two wars), young Iain was impressed by the fact that the dinner gong was 'a piper playing up and then down the antler-avenued Long Passage'. He also formed a fascination for the grotesque set of paintings depicting the various stages of drunkenness in the Guard Room. These were acquired from a drinking club on the Isle of Man – of which the Dukes of Atholl inherited the sovereignty from the Stanleys.

Besides the multifarious treasures of Blair it is such idiosyncratic memorabilia that constantly divert one's attention. Almost everywhere you browse at Blair there is an evocative vignette – whether a group photograph in 1886 of the estate stalkers on the hill, every one of them sporting a luxuriant beard, or the romantic, tartan-covered bedroom on the second floor commemorating the Jacobite Murrays.

Among the more bizarre exhibits are a coronet made of deer's teeth set in enamel, man-traps and a bewildering array of stuffed birds in the natural history

ABOVE The west front. The standard of the Dukes of Atholl flies from the tower.

LEFT The Tapestry Room, dominated by its splendid late 17th-century bed, hung with red Spitalfields silk and surmounted by four plumes of ostrich feathers. This theatrical extravaganza was formerly in the Holyrood house apartment of the 1st Duke of Atholl – who also acquired the Brussels tapestries in the room (made for King Charles I and sold by Oliver Cromwell).

museum ranging from an albatross and a bustard to a duck-billed platypus. A caption describing a grouse of 'abnormal colour' explains that its mate was also shot on August 12, 1884, 'but Cook plucked it'.

Happily, the family connection has not – contrary to misleading reports in the press following the death of 'Wee Iain', the 10th Duke of Atholl, in 1996 when the title passed to a South African kinsman – been 'plucked' from the castle, which somehow, despite the legions of visitors, retains the atmosphere of a private house. 'Wee Iain', a shy, gentle bachelor bolstered by the Pearson fortune of his mother, a daughter of the 2nd Viscount Cowdray, managed to secure Blair's future before his untimely death by setting up a charitable trust. His half-sister, Sarah Troughton, maintains a family presence at Blair; the great ancestral acres of the Atholls are in safe hands; and the artistic and political tensions inherent in the castle have been peacefully resolved.

2

GLAMIS CASTLE

ANGUS

L ONG before Lady Elizabeth Bowes Lyon (now Queen Elizabeth The Queen Mother) married the future King George VI, the Earls of Strathmore were one of the most famous of the great families of Scotland, on account of their long and colourful history and the bloodcurdling legends – the secret room and all the rest of it – associated with their ancestral seat of Glamis. With its massive tower and cluster of pointed turrets, Glamis could be said to be everybody's idea of a Scottish castle, yet in architectural terms this amazing pink apparition at the climax of a wide avenue of oaks is really remarkably unusual – 'very singular and striking in appearance, like nothing I ever saw', as the poet Thomas Gray put it when he stayed here in 1765.

And for all its medieval core and castellated facade, Glamis is also undeniably a 'great house', with glorious 17th-century plasterwork and furniture, as well as almost untouched, and highly atmospheric, 19th-century decoration. Indeed, when it comes to atmosphere Glamis is surely in a class of its own. Nearly 30 years after Gray's visit another writer, the great Sir Walter Scott, came to stay at Glamis as a young man and noted:

> After a very hospitable reception ... I was conducted to my
> apartments in a distant part of the building. I must own that when
> I heard door after door shut, after my conductor had retired, I
> began to consider myself too far from the living, and somewhat too
> near the dead ... The heavy pile contains much in its appearance,
> and in the tradition connected with it, impressive to the
> imagination. It was the scene of the murder of a Scottish King of
> great antiquity, not indeed the gracious Duncan, with whom the
> name naturally associates itself, but Malcolm II. The extreme
> antiquity of the building is vouched by the thickness of the walls
> and the wild straggling arrangement of the accommodation within

doors…In spite of the truth of history, the whole night scene in Macbeth's Castle rushed at once upon me and struck my mind more forcibly than even when I have seen its terrors represented by John Kemble and his inimitable sister [Mrs Siddons, the actress].

As Scott says, the Shakespearean associations ('This castle hath a pleasant seat; the air/Nimbly and sweetly recommends itself/Unto our gentle senses') are purely fanciful, though there is good authority that King Malcolm II, Duncan's grandfather, met his death at Glamis in 1034. In those days Glamis was a royal hunting lodge and so it remained until the 14th century when Robert II, the first Stuart King of Scots, granted the Thaneage of Glamis to Sir John Lyon of Forteviot in 1372. 'The White Lyon', as he was known (presumably on account of his fair hair and pale skin), went on to marry the King's daughter, Princess Jean, or 'Joanna', four years later and to be appointed Chamberlain of Scotland.

It was the White Lyon's son, also Sir John, who began building the east wing of the present castle in the early 15th century. In the next generation the 1st Lord Glamis began work on the Great Tower in about 1435. This was completed by his widow, though it was not linked to the east wing for a further hundred years.

PRECEDING PAGES View of the castle from the east, looking up from the Dutch Garden.

ABOVE The ubiquitous Glamis lion.

LEFT Gateway to the Dutch Garden laid out by the 13th Earl of Strathmore in 1893.

RIGHT The winding spiral staircase in the castle's central turret, which was remodelled by the 2nd Earl of Kinghorne in the early 17th century.

ABOVE 'My great hall which is a room that I have ever loved,' wrote the 3rd Earl of Strathmore, portrayed in Classical costume by the prolific Jacob de Wet in the conversation piece which dominates the far end of what is now the Drawing Room. The castle's finest 17th-century interior, it has a barrel-vaulted ceiling and an armorial overmantel. The modern wooden screen, to the left, is by Viscount Linley, whose mother, Princess Margaret, was born at Glamis in 1930.

LEFT The 3rd Earl of Strathmore strikes a Classical pose as he shows off both his torso (in remarkably revealing body armour) and, underneath his right hand, the castle he remodelled in the late 17th century.

In the 16th century another widow of a subsequent Lord Glamis, the 6th, was to play a tragic role in Glamis's history. Poor Janet Douglas had the misfortune to be the sister of the Earl of Angus, whose stepson King James V determined to destroy any Douglases he could lay his hands on. In 1537 Lady Glamis and her second husband, Archibald Campbell of Skipnish, were duly sentenced to death on a trumped-up charge of sorcery. Campbell, attempting to escape from Edinburgh Castle, was dashed to pieces by falling rocks, and the innocent Janet, virtually blind after languishing in a dark dungeon, was burnt as a witch on Castle Hill. Her gentle spirit is said to haunt the Chapel at Glamis.

The dastardly James V declared Glamis forfeit to the Crown and helped himself to the Lyon possessions. The records show, for instance, that 12 great silver flagons were melted down to supply silver for the Royal Mint. On one of the King's visits the royal party tucked into 54 capons, 90 chickens and 24 geese.

Yet only 20 years after James's death – by one of those moral somersaults so prevalent in Scottish family sagas – Janet's grandson, the 8th Lord Glamis, was entertaining the King's daughter, Mary Queen of Scots, at the castle. The English ambassador, who was of the party, reported to Queen Elizabeth I that in spite of 'extreme Fowle and Colde weather, I never saw her merrier, never dismayed'. Mary's ladies-in-waiting spent their time making a new tapestry chair cover – hardly adequate recompense, it might be thought, for James V's depredations.

The 8th Lord Glamis, who was Chancellor of Scotland and Keeper of the Great Seal, had – according to the English Ambassador – 'the greatest revenue of any baron in Scotland'. The household consisted of 'a principal servitor and maister stabular, 2 servitors, a musicianer, master cook and browster, foremen, a maister porter and his servant, a grieve and an officer'. The lady of the house was attended by '2 gentlewomen, a browdinstar [embroiderer], a lotrix [bedmaker] and two other female servants'.

The family fortunes, however, were depleted by their involvement in the Covenanting (against popery and episcopacy) troubles of the 17th century. It was said that the 2nd Earl of Kinghorne – whose father, the 9th Lord Glamis, remodelled the castle tower and stair turret and was created an Earl in 1606 – came to his inheritance the richest peer in Scotland and left it the poorest. His decision to help finance the Covenanting army against his former friend the Marquess of Montrose resulted in debts amounting to £40,000 – a staggering sum in those days.

The 3rd Earl (who had the designation of his peerage changed to that of 'Earl of Strathmore and Kinghorne') was advised that his estates were 'irrecoverable'. Matters were not improved by the Cromwellian occupation of Glamis. When he finally took up residence with his wife in 1670 – lodging in the only glazed rooms at the top of the great stair – prospects were bleak indeed.

Nonetheless, it is to this Lord Strathmore that Glamis owes most today. With admirable determination he managed to pay off the debts and then proceeded to remodel the castle over the next 20 years. From his *Book of Record* (preserved at Glamis) he emerges as a man of taste and a most sympathetic figure. A.H. Millar, who edited the Earl's diary for the Scottish Historical Society, summed him up as:

> A man of strict integrity and uprightness, with a profound respect
> for the honour of his ancestors and a deep sense of his
> responsibility for posterity…just without penuriousness, generous
> with discretion, affectionate in the family circle, and tender and
> true to his friends and relatives…mild and amiable.

LEFT The Billiard Room, which dates from the 18th century but has a ceiling of 1903 installed to mark the Golden Wedding of the 13th Earl of Strathmore and his Countess. The fireplace came from a Bowes property, Gibside, Co. Durham; the Bowes Lyon banner hangs above, flanked by colours of the 2nd Battalion Scots Guards.

RIGHT The sideboard alcove of the Victorian Dining Room with portraits of the 13th Earl of Strathmore and his Countess (the former Frances Smith).

LEFT The Biblical scenes on the ceiling panels of the Chapel, by Jacob de Wet, are thought to have been based on engravings by Boetius a Bolswert, dated 1622. De Wet's brief was to conform to scenes in the 3rd Earl of Strathmore's Bible – the Flight into Egypt, the Last Supper, and so on.

ABOVE The Chapel: a remarkable late 17th-century survival, sensitively restored by the 13th Earl of Strathmore in 1866 and dedicated to St Michael and All Angels. The wall paintings, by de Wet, were based on engravings by Jacquet Callot of 1631. De Wet received £90 for his efforts in 1688.

It is particularly endearing to see that he kept a 'private buffoon', or jester, at Glamis – the last household to do so in Scotland. The silken suit of motley can still be seen in the Drawing Room and somehow epitomizes the zest and gaiety that outshines the ghostly gloom of the castle. It would seem that Lord Strathmore was his own architect. As he noted in his diary:

> Tho' it be an old house and consequentlie was the more difficult to
> reduce the place to any uniformitie yet did I covet extremely to
> order my building so that my frontispiece might have a resemblance
> on both syds, and my Great Hall haveing no following was also a
> great inducement to me for reering up that quarter upon the west
> syd wah now is, haveing first founded it, I built my walls according
> to my draught.

In 1679 he added the west wing, and so modified the typically Scottish 'L'-shape of the old tower, and heightened the central block to give Glamis its highly distinctive roof-line. He placed the stone armorials on the face of the staircase tower, where his own portrait bust also appears. This and lead statues of Kings James VI and Charles I on either side of the avenue are by Arnold Quellin.

The avenue was laid out at an angle of 45 degrees to the castle so that the large stair became the centre of the composition. The courtyard buildings were swept away and in front Lord Strathmore created a baroque setting of courts, sculptures and vistas.

Inside, he cleverly transformed 'My Great Hall, which is a room that I ever loved' into the delightful barrel-vaulted Drawing Room, preserving the handsome plasterwork installed in 1621 by his father, the 2nd Earl of Kinghorne. The pretty pink walls are hung with family portraits, dominated by a group study of Lord Strathmore (in a curious 'see-through' tunic) with his sons and dogs.

Another fine interior created by the 3rd Earl is the Chapel, consecrated in 1688, a fascinating survival of a decorative scheme from the time of Archbishop Laud. Both ceiling and walls are copiously covered by panels painted by the Dutch artist Jacob de Wet (who made up in prolific output for what he may have lacked in talent), depicting the Life of Christ and the Twelve Apostles.

In 1716 – the year after the first Jacobite Rising, in which the young 5th Earl of Strathmore was killed at Sheriffmuir while fighting for the Stuart cause – 'the Old Chevalier' (or, in Sassenach speak, 'the Old Pretender'), otherwise King James VIII and III, 'touched' for the King's Evil in this chapel. That is to say, he laid hands on local sufferers from a lymphatic disorder, all of whom – so it is said – promptly recovered.

The Old Chevalier left behind a couple of items at Glamis – one deliberately, the other accidentally. His sword (inscribed 'God save King James VIII, prosperitie to Scotland, and no union') can be seen in the Family Exhibition, as now can the other object, a watch inadvertently forgotten under the Old Chevalier's pillow. The story goes that a maid stole it but many years later the light-fingered one's descendant returned the timepiece to Glamis.

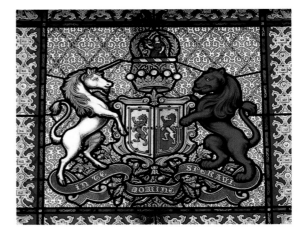

Heraldic stained-glass window in the Dining Room.

There are also to be found diverting memorabilia in the Billiard Room, one of the improvements (together with new kitchens and service courts) added by the 9th Earl of Strathmore. This Earl effectively restored the family fortunes by marrying the rich Durham heiress Mary Eleanor Bowes, though after his death she was abducted by a scoundrel called Stoney who ended his days within the 'Rules' of the King's Bench Prison.

The 10th Earl lived mainly on his Durham estates – his illegitimate son, John Bowes, founded the amazing Frenchified Bowes Museum at Barnard Castle – but carried on his father's improvements at Glamis, including the rebuilding of the west wing. This wing contains the impressively 'Jacobethan' Dining Room: a stately 19th-century ensemble of heraldically embossed ceiling, chimneypiece and dado, armorial glass and even fire-dogs.

The castle was modernized again at the end of the 19th century by the 13th Earl of Strathmore. In the next generation, the 14th Earl's brood of nine surviving children are evocatively portrayed in an exquisitely Edwardian conversation piece on an easel in the corner of the Drawing Room. The youngest, Lady Elizabeth, prophetically known as 'Princess', enchanted the wounded soldiers convalescing at Glamis during the First World War when her mother, Lady Strathmore, turned the castle into a hospital. 'May you be hung, drawn and quartered,' wrote one waggish military man in Lady Elizabeth's autograph book, no less prophetically. 'Yes, hung in diamonds, drawn in coach and four, and quartered in the best house in the land.'

The Queen Mother's presence is particularly potent in the Royal Apartments at Glamis, which were set aside for her use by her mother in 1923 following her marriage to the Duke of York. The consummately cosy corner sitting room contains childhood photographs of the two Princesses, Elizabeth and Margaret – who was born at Glamis in 1930.

As well as being the first royal birth in the direct line since the future King Charles I's at Dunfermline in 1600, it was also the last occasion when a Government minister was required to be present at a royal birth (to prevent any baby-swapping). Following the somewhat farcical to-ings and fro-ings of the

King James VI of Scotland (and I of England), sculpted by Arnold Quellin, surveys the massive entrance front of Glamis Castle.

Labour Home Secretary, a Mr J.R. Clynes (who pronounced the infant Princess to be 'a fine chubby-faced little girl'), the antiquated practice was finally discontinued.

Princess Margaret's craftsman son, Viscount Linley, executed the ambitious marquetry screen depicting the castle in various woods which is now an attractive feature of the Drawing Room. Such a refreshingly modern touch is a pleasing reminder that Glamis is still very much a vital, breathing late-20th-century family home. Lord Linley's cousin and near-contemporary, the 18th and present Earl of Strathmore and Kinghorne, still lives here with his wife and young family.

Despite the unbeatable historic allure of Glamis, not to mention – and it *isn't* mentioned – the hoary old nonsense of 'the Monster', it is the friendly spirit generated by recent generations of the Bowes Lyon family that makes the strongest impression amid the baronial baroque. The title of the sheet music on the piano in the Billiard Room sets the tone of the place – 'Just Snap Your Fingers at Dull Care' – conjuring up paradisal images of the Queen Mother's favourite author, P.G. Wodehouse.

3

DRUMLANRIG CASTLE

DUMFRIESSHIRE

THANKS to Mel Gibson's colourful, if – to say the least – historically unreliable, film, the romantic phrase 'Brave Heart' has recently rung resonantly around the world as a symbol of Scotland. In reality, or at least much better-founded tradition, the symbolism is rooted in the story of Sir James Douglas, 'The Good' or 'Black Douglas', a stalwart supporter of King Robert Bruce in the early 14th century. Robert Bruce died, in 1329, before he could achieve his ambition of going on Crusade to the Holy Land so the Black Douglas was entrusted with the King's heart when he himself went off to fight the Infidel. As Douglas fell mortally wounded in a battle with the Moors in Spain he is said to have hurled the royal heart (contained in a silver casket) before him with the truly epic cry: 'Forward, brave heart!'

The Douglas crest duly became a winged heart surmounted by Bruce's crown and it is this heraldic emblem that constantly catches the eye on a visit to the spectacular family seat of Drumlanrig Castle, home of the 9th Duke of Buccleuch and 11th Duke of Queensberry. The 'brave heart' (together with the motto, 'Forward') is everywhere: in stone, lead, iron, wood, leather, carpeting and so forth.

The romance needs no Hollywood burnish for surely there can be few more romantic places in the world than Drumlanrig in its dramatic Border landscape glowing pink in the twilight. Framed by skilfully planted woods and surrounded by the glorious green slopes of Nithsdale, the sensationally dramatic castle cries out for the brush of, say, Claude – one of the few great masters not to be represented on the walls within. No amount of anticipation can prepare one for the impact experienced at the climax of the ingeniously devised approach. The boldness and grandeur of this Renaissance composition rob one of breath.

Facing you is a noble facade of late-Stuart Baroque which almost outdoes (and pre-dates) Sir John Vanbrugh for sheer splendour and exuberance. The eye feasts on a curving perron, an arcaded loggia, giant pilasters, balustrades and rows of pedimented windows and soars upwards to savour the cluster of turrets decorating the four corner towers. Then you find yourself focusing on the exquisitely adorned porch with its trophies and coats of arms. Phew, this is architecture all right.

Yet, as so often with well executed good ideas, the overall effect is surprisingly simple and straightforward. The plan, after all, derives from the castles of the later Middle Ages. Indeed traces of the original Douglas stronghold dating from the 14th and 15th centuries are still discernible and the present great house – one of the foremost Renaissance buildings in the grand manner in Scottish domestic architecture – was effectively superimposed on the old castle.

The Barony of Drumlanrig was originally a property of the Earls of Mar, whose heiress had married the 1st Earl of Douglas, progenitor of a powerful Lowland dynasty whose vast landholdings were to stretch over much of Scotland by the end of the 14th century. The 2nd Earl of Douglas (and Mar), who was killed at the Battle of Otterburn in 1388, had a natural son, William, to whom he bequeathed Drumlanrig. The rest of the Douglas territorial empire, and the titles, passed to the Black Douglas's son, Archibald. This probably helped the Drumlanrig line to maintain a reasonably low profile, and to survive. Son succeeded father in the Douglas male line at Drumlanrig for nearly 400 years.

This branch of the Douglases was also shrewd enough to support the Crown even, as at the Battle of Lochmaben in 1484, against the Earls of Douglas. A charter of King James III regranted the Baronies of Drumlanrig and Hawick to be held 'in Chief of the crown, not of the Earl of Douglas, as Formerly'. The 6th Laird (whose mother was a Scott of Buccleuch) fell at Flodden beside

PRECEDING PAGES View of Drumlanrig Castle from Mount Malloch.

Early morning light on the north (entrance) front, with cattle in attendance.

ABOVE 'Brave heart': detail of stonework.

RIGHT Roofscape.

King James IV, though Sir James Douglas, the 7th Laird and guardian of the Western Marches, managed to earn the disapproval of Mary Queen of Scots. She included the meddlesome old schemer in her celebrated list of 'the hell houndis, bloody tyrantis, without soullis or feir of God'.

Nonetheless, Mary's son, King James VI and I, was entertained at Drumlanrig in 1617 and the laird of the day, Sir William Douglas, could take satisfaction from the old saw, 'He who stands on the Hassock hill/Shall rule all Nithsdale at his will'. Sir William rose to become Viscount Drumlanrig and, in 1633, Earl of Queensberry; in his grandson's time the Douglases of Drumlanrig advanced still further, to a dukedom.

The 3rd Earl and 1st Duke of Queensberry continued the family's staunch adherence to the House of Stuart, even though his own religious views were Episcopalian while those of Kings Charles II and James VII and II veered towards Roman Catholicism. As Lord High Treasurer of Scotland, Duke William became the most powerful man in the country and decided that his family needed a more fitting pile than the old castle (probably the second on the site) in which James VI had been feted on his return to Scotland.

LEFT View through the Drawing Room, showing Grinling Gibbons's carving above the door.

RIGHT Staircase Hall: the oak staircase and balustrade was one of the first of its kind in Scotland.

BELOW Detail of Grinling Gibbons's carving in the Drawing Room.

A man of artistic tastes, Duke William is said, as *The Complete Peerage* notes, to have 'well-nigh ruined himself' in his ambitious rebuilding operations between 1679 and 1691. His architect is not known for certain, though the most likely candidate seems to be James Smith, son-in-law of Robert Mylne, the King's Master Mason (who may also have had a hand in the design). The master of works, or builder, is, however, on record: William Lukup (buried in the nearby Durisdeer Church).

Whoever was responsible for the designs of the new Drumlanrig must have had access to the drawings made earlier in the 17th century when a remodelling of the old castle was first contemplated. Sir William Bruce, the great gentleman amateur, was the architect consulted then. This provenance gives a clue as to why the style is slightly 'out of date' for the 1680s and more reminiscent of Heriot's Hospital in Edinburgh, which was built in the 1620s.

Built of local pink sandstone, Duke William's house was constructed round an open courtyard, with a circular staircase tower in each corner. Two Dutchmen, Peter Paul Boyse and Cornelius Van Nerven (who had worked for Bruce at Kinross – *qv*), carried out the elaborate stone carving. Inside, there

was the innovation of a passage linking rooms, while the magnificent oak staircase and balustrade was one of the first of its kind in Scotland. The fine wooden overmantels and overdoors are thought to be by Grinling Gibbons; they are certainly in his style.

In short, no expense was spared, not forgetting the laying-out of elaborate formal gardens. Duke William came to regret his extravagance. Sir Walter Scott relates that the Duke folded up the accounts of Drumlanrig in a sealed parcel, with a label bidding 'the deil pike out the een of any of my successors that shall open it'. Today, though, one can only salute his memory.

Some Jacobites tended to be less respectful towards his son, known to history as 'the Union Duke'. George Lockhart waxed indignant: 'The son, notwithstanding King Charles and King James's kindness to his father and family... was the first Scotsman that deserted over to the Prince of Orange, and from thence acquir'd the epithet (amongst honest men) of Proto-rebel'. The doubtless honest Sir Herbert Maxwell, however, maintained of the Union Duke's role in carrying the Act through that 'the statesman who should undertake this formidable task had need not only of moral fortitude and conviction, but of personal courage'.

The Ante-Room, with a late 17th-century Brussels tapestry and an early 18th-century Flemish ebony cabinet (with gilt metalwork), probably brought over by the Duke of Monmouth – whose wife, Anne, Duchess of Buccleuch, is portrayed above it. The centre table is in the style of Boulle.

A corner of the Drawing Room, showing the cabinet made for Louis XIV's Versailles and a full-length portrait of King James VI's Queen, Anne of Denmark, attributed to George Jamesone.

The Act of Union also indirectly caused a ghastly episode in the history of the Douglas family. The Union Duke had an unhinged son who was kept locked up in a cell at Holyrood, but during the debates on the Union this dangerous Earl of Drumlanrig was left unguarded while the servants went out to see the riots in Edinburgh. He escaped from his confinement and fell upon a cookboy, who was turning the spit in the kitchen. After killing the boy Lord Drumlanrig then proceeded to truss the corpse up on the spit and roast it before the fire. Fortunately, the 'Cannibalistic Idiot', who predeceased his father, had already been passed over in the entail of the estates.

His brother, the 3rd Duke, happily upheld the best traditions of the family and proved an understanding husband to his somewhat wild and eccentric Duchess, Kitty, the patroness of her secretary, John Gay of *Beggar's Opera* fame. When Horace Walpole proposed a toast wishing that the Duchess 'might live to grow ugly', the witty Kitty responded, 'I hope, then, you will keep your taste for antiquities.'

The tastes of the next Duke, the notorious rake 'Old Q' or 'the Goat of Piccadilly', were principally concentrated on ogling the girls from his vantage point on a balcony near Hyde Park Corner in London. In Old Q's youth Thomas Pelham, the Prime Minister, had (according to the diarist Wraxall) rejected him

LEFT Bonnie Prince Charlie's Bedroom, occupied by Prince Charles Edward, 'the Young Pretender', on his retreat north on December 22, 1745. His supporters showed their dislike for King William III by lacerating his equestrian portrait in the Staircase Hall. The tapestries on the wall are late-17th-century Brussels, and the painting over the chimneypiece is probably by Nicholas Heude, a French artist brought to Scotland from London by the 1st Duke of Queensberry.

ABOVE Cherubic closeness: detail of one of Drumlanrig's many fine carvings.

as a possible son-in-law 'considering him a nobleman of dissipated habits, character and fortune'. He did not improve and the Drumlanrig estate, shamefully neglected, declined with him – or rather without him as the old reprobate remained in the fleshpots of London.

When Old Q finally expired ('of a severe flux') in 1810, aged 85, the Dukedom and the Marquessate of Queensberry went in different directions. The Dukedom passed to the 3rd Duke of Buccleuch (whose grandmother was the Union Duke's daughter), while the Marquessate was inherited by a Douglas kinsman, great-uncle of Oscar Wilde's 'Screaming Scarlet Marquess', and Old Q's cash (derived from the sale of Drumlanrig's trees) went to his illegitimate daughter, who married the 3rd Marquess of Hertford, thereby helping to fund the Wallace Collection.

The 3rd Duke of Buccleuch – a descendant of the dashing Duke of Monmouth (King Charles II's son by Lucy Walters) who married the heiress of the long-established Border family, the Scotts of Buccleuch – not only came into the Douglas Dukedom of Queensberry and the Drumlanrig estate but also married the eventual heiress of the English Dukes of Montagu. Consequently Drumlanrig's contents were enhanced by the combined treasures of the Montagus and Scotts, on top of those of the Douglases.

The 4th Duke of Buccleuch (and 6th Duke of Queensberry) inherited the Drumlanrig estate in 1812 and embarked on an ambitious programme to repair the depredations wrought by Old Q, with copious advice from his close friend and kinsman Sir Walter Scott. His son, Walter Francis, succeeded him seven years later at the age of 12. As 5th Duke, he proved to be a public-spirited

ABOVE The Duke of Buccleuch at Drumlanrig.

LEFT View of Drumlanrig from Mount Malloch, with snow on mountains.

agriculturalist and philanthropist, who replanted woodlands, modernized farmsteads and transformed Drumlanrig into the thriving rural estate it remains today.

It was also in the early part of the 19th century that the castle underwent various changes. The formerly open loggia was glazed when it became the entrance lobby, and the original hall was converted into a dining room. The long gallery, above the loggia, was divided, on Sir Walter Scott's suggestion, into bedrooms. Plaster ceilings and new panelling were also installed in several parts of the house, though most of the late 17th-century interiors were happily left undisturbed.

To bring the story up to date, a 20-year programme of renewing all the lead roofing, including the rebuilding of all the little cupolas, was completed in 1995 – without, as the present Duke points out, any Government grants. The repair and replacement of the stone carvings, some of which had crumbled away beyond recognition, are well advanced but at least another dozen years will be needed. The pace of progress depends upon the estate's farms and forests continuing to provide the necessary finance despite such setbacks as BSE and fluctuating timber prices. This, as the Duke says, 'demonstrates the importance of the cohesion between an historic house and its surrounding countryside'.

The fabulous treasures of Drumlanrig – intensified to an even greater degree since the closure this century of two of the family's other seats, Dalkeith (near Edinburgh) and Montagu House (in London) – would soon exhaust descriptive superlatives. The furniture embraces French and English masterpieces from royal palaces; there are Chippendale wall sconces, ormolu-mounted Sèvres, and, in the room in which Bonnie Prince Charlie slept on his retreat from Derby, a beautifully embroidered Carolean bedcover.

As for the pictures, a remark made by the present Duke of Buccleuch as he enthusiastically showed us round speaks volumes. 'If you lie on your back underneath the 1670s silver chandelier on the staircase,' he encouraged the photographer, 'it must be the only place in the world where you can see simultaneously a Rembrandt, a Holbein and a Leonardo da Vinci.' For many visitors to Drumlanrig, Rembrandt's *Old Woman Reading* (1655), with its astonishingly delicate use of light, ranks as the finest painting they have ever seen.

The Boudoir shows off Dutch cabinet paintings to good effect while Old Q by Allan Ramsay can be found in the Dining Room. The plethora of family portraits are brought up to date by a charming 1950s study of the present Duchess by John Merton in the Morning Room. This is a pleasing reminder that Drumlanrig is still a much-loved family home at the centre of a flourishing community, rightly celebrated for its contributions to countryside management and education (Dr David Bellamy has described the Duke's property as 'the best-managed estates in the world').

The close links within that world are nicely reflected in the set of household portraits by John Ainslie in the Serving Room – including one of the remarkable chef, Joseph Florence, whose culinary arts were appreciated by three successive Dukes and by Sir Walter Scott rather in the manner of Bertie Wooster admiring Anatole at Aunt Dahlia's.

The Master would doubtless have relished the present Duke's anecdote about his late mother's terror of bats. One night she was set upon by some of these creatures as she walked through the darkness of the hall. 'Help! Bats!' she shrieked, as she ran round and round in circles to escape their attention. 'Bats! *Bats*!' Whereupon a sepulchral voice sounded from the gloom: 'You called, Your Grace?' It was the family butler, Mr Batts. No Hollywood scriptwriter could improve on that.

4

CAWDOR
CASTLE

*T*HE familiar Shakespearean quotation 'This castle hath a pleasant seat ...' which was invoked in the chapter on Glamis (*qv*) also tends to be bandied about in association with Cawdor Castle further north. This is hardly surprising as the two Thanes mentioned in *Macbeth* are those of Glamis and Cawdor, or rather 'Cawder'. Yet, as the late Earl Cawdor pointed out in his deliciously salty and witty guide-book to the castle – undoubtedly the most entertaining and instructive example of that often dismally dull genre – Macbeth himself died in 1052 whereas the 1st Thane of Cawdor did not flourish until the end of the 13th century.

'The truth is,' the sharp and scholarly Hugh Cawdor wrote, 'that as Cawdor Castle was not built until the late 14th century, it is impossible for King Duncan to have lost any blood or Lady Macbeth much sleep in this house.' One can sympathize with the exasperated explanation of the 5th Earl (Hugh's father): 'I wish the Bard had never written his damned play.' Nonetheless, haunting Shakespearean overtones somehow cling to this wonderfully atmospheric castle, with its great medieval tower and old drawbridge (the only one extant at a privately inhabited castle in Scotland), brooding above dark Cawdor burn. Paradoxically, though, the castle is also far from a fortress in character: it is a great house of intimacy and charm surrounded by delightful gardens and serene parkland. In architectural terms it is a perfect instance of a Scots 'compound' great house: 14th-century great keep, 15th-century fortifications; 17th-century domestic additions.

Even if the *Macbeth* legend does not – to borrow one of Hugh Cawdor's colourful phrases – 'hold Scotch mist, let alone water', the tradition of the castle's building is inevitably romantic. The story goes that the 3rd Thane of Cawdor, who had a small castle about a mile away, decided to build a stronger tower on a higher, harder site and that this new situation was chosen not by an architect but by a donkey ('creatures with much in common', as Hugh

Cawdor put it). For the Thane had a dream. As instructed by his subconscious, he duly loaded a coffer of gold on to the back of a donkey and let it roam about the district for a day. The theory was that wherever the animal lay down to rest in the evening, there the Thane's castle would be sited and it would prosper for evermore. Presumably to the Thane's chagrin, the ass lay down beneath a tree.

Nothing daunted, the Thane followed his dream and constructed the new castle around the tree. Although the British Isles boast several bizarre houses in trees – one thinks, for example, of the one at Pitchford Hall in Shropshire – Cawdor must be the only case of a tree in a house. However much dry-as-dust architectural historians may sniff over these sorts of fancy yarns, in the stout central vault of the old tower there is still the astonishing sight of an ancient tree trunk. For centuries it was assumed to be a hawthorn; the vault, or ground-floor guardroom (which protected the approaches to the drawbridge and contains a secret dungeon concealed in the thickness of the end wall), is known as the Thorn Tree Room.

In fact, microscopic analysis of the wood has identified the tree as a holly. Otherwise, though, modern scientific methods have tended to confirm rather than deny the legend. Radiocarbon measurement dates the wood of the tree to about 1372 – the last quarter of the 14th century in which the building of the castle has always thought to have begun even if the academics who demand documentary evidence for everything prefer to cite the date of the building licence, 1454.

This Special Licence to fortify was granted by King James II to his friend the 6th Thane of Cawdor, Crown Chamberlain beyond the Spey, with a significant reference to 'the perfection and completion of the said Castle [of Cawdor]'. It seems reasonable to infer that a new castle of sorts already existed.

The original tower-house – tall, plain, rectangular – would have comprised four storeys and a garret, served by a turnpike stair. There was only one entrance to the outside world set at upper first floor level – 'the perfect design to keep out tourists' as Hugh Cawdor observes in the castle guide-book. The entrance arch is still clearly visible in the masonry on the east front.

The tower-house would have been surrounded by a curtain wall within which the Thane's clansmen could take refuge. This wall has long since disappeared;

PRECEDING PAGES 'An ancient, honourable and agreeable seat...': Cawdor by floodlight. The banner of the Campbells, Earls and Thanes of Cawdor flies above the 14th-century great keep.

Wintry view of the back of the castle from the burn.

ABOVE Corner of north courtyard.

ABOVE RIGHT Pepper-pot turret on the roof of a crenellated tower.

BELOW The arms of Sir Hugh Campbell, the 15th Thane, quartered with those of his wife, Lady Henrietta Stuart, dated 1672 (the year that all coats of arms had to be registered for approval by the Lord Lyon King of Arms). It was the 15th Thane who transformed the old fortress into a great house – thereby exchanging, as the 25th Thane put it, the hospitality on offer from boiling oil to mulled claret.

the attractive building with crow-stepped gables about the little courtyards to the east and north dates, in the main, from the 17th century when Cawdor Castle took on a more domestic character. Today the main entrance to the castle is approached through the little north courtyard which displays the coat of arms of the 15th Thane, Sir Hugh Campbell, and leads into the additions which he built.

The present Campbells of Cawdor descend from a remarkable forced union (what Hugh Cawdor typically called a 'crossbow wedding') at the beginning of the 16th century. By the end of the 15th century the denizens of the castle, who had married well, were beginning to live up to the image of *Macbeth* in which the Thane of Cawdor is described as a 'prosperous Gentleman'. So much so that in 1498 the greedy 2nd Earl of Argyll, the most influential man in Scotland at the time, decided to kidnap the posthumous baby daughter of his kinsman the 8th Thane of Cawdor. The wretched infant Muriel was branded on the hip with a red-hot key and the top joint of the little finger of her left hand was bitten off. These barbarities were perpetrated in order to ensure Muriel's future recognition, though Lord Argyll appears to have been not unduly worried about any risk of mistaken identity. When it was pointed out to him that the little girl might die and therefore the loss of his clansmen in abducting her (half-a-dozen Campbells of Inverliever, who had been guarding, by way of a decoy, a sheaf of corn dressed up in the baby's clothes, were killed by a pursuing posse of Cawdor stalwarts) would be wasted, Argyll's legendary response chilled the blood. Muriel of Cawdor, he said, would never die as long as there was 'a red-headed Lassie on the banks of Loch Awe' (or Loch Fyne, according to which version of the tale you prefer).

In 1510, at the age of 12, Muriel was duly married to Argyll's younger son, Sir John Campbell. Curiously enough, as 'arranged' nuptials often seem to do, the marriage worked well enough. After a tempestuous start on the Muckairn estate in Argyll – which culminated in Sir John stabbing his brother-in-law, Lachlan Maclean, to death after this disagreeable neighbour had chained

Cleaning the grille, in keeping with the Thanes' family motto displayed above the entrance archway: 'BE MINDFUL'.

ABOVE Detail of robust chimneypiece of 1607 in private sitting room.

the naked Lady Elizabeth to a tidal skerry – the Campbells headed north-east for Cawdor. Once some disgruntled uncles of Muriel had been summarily disposed of, Sir John consolidated the estate and the subsequent Thanes became almost too powerful for their own good.

The 11th Thane was blown away by a blunderbuss in a clan feud; the 12th Thane overreached himself by buying the island of Islay; and the unfortunate 13th Thane, 'the fiar', was certified insane, a condition possibly not unconnected with his wife's habit of poisoning the victuals. The morning after one jolly supper party at Cawdor three guests were found dead in their beds.

Happily, at last the house was put literally in order by the lunatic's nephew, Sir Hugh Campbell, the 15th Thane, who preferred to mind his own business and devote himself to the sporting pleasures of the chase. Together with his wife, Lady Henrietta Stuart (daughter of the 3rd Earl of Moray from neighbouring Darnaway Castle), Sir Hugh succeeded in transforming the forbidding old fortress of Cawdor into a comfortable great house between 1684 and 1702. As his descendant and namesake put it, 'Whereas his ancestors had set the castle out in such a way as to give marauders a hot reception with boiling oil and molten lead, he could now rest happily at ease and grant his friends a warm welcome with mulled claret beside a glowing hearth.'

The windows became larger, robust fireplaces were installed, and splendid beds and tapestries brought in. A strange little tower, which had stood at the north-east corner of the Old Hall, was demolished; a new library wing was added complete with a balustrade echoing the Palladian principles of Sir Hugh's nephew, the celebrated architect Colen Campbell; and the whole composition of the castle was neatly tidied up so that, in the words of the building contract, the craftsmen completed everything in 'handsomest order, so as themselves may have credit and Sir Hugh satisfaction'.

Yet in the troubled times after the first Jacobite Rising and the death of Sir Hugh (who had nobly declared his hand for the Stuart cause) the following year, there was to be little mulled claret at Cawdor. The Thanes wisely

RIGHT The Tower Room: Flemish tapestries, eclectic pictures and furniture, such as the 18th-century Venetian gondola seat in the foreground. Note the thickness of the wall in the window recess to the left. The door on the right led to a medieval closet (in the most basic sense of that euphemism).

decamped to their Welsh estates for the next century, leaving Cawdor to the care of factors – though in the 1720s Sir Hugh's younger son, Sir Archibald Campbell, carried out various improvements including the creation of the upper garden.

Neglect of an old house can be a joyful preservative. Cawdor was consequently spared the fashionable changes of the 18th century; and fortunately the 19th century, when the Thanes returned, proved much more in sympathy with the castle's spirit. Some essential building work was necessary after a fire in 1819 which devastated the middle storeys of the tower. The 1st Earl Cawdor (whose father, the 1st Lord Cawdor, was celebrated for accepting the surrender

BELOW The Tapestry Bedroom, the 'best bedroom' above the great hall, which was done up for the 15th Thane's marriage in 1662 to Lady Henrietta Stuart at the nearby Darnaway Castle. Their marriage-bed has been restored with crimson velvet hangings and white feathers in accordance with Lady Henrietta's housekeeping notebook of 1688 ('In the Crimson Chamber there is a Crimson velvet bed...'). The Flemish tapestries were brought over in 1682. They show what the 25th Thane called scenes of 'Old Testament peevishness', as well as of the chase so beloved by the 15th Thane, 'a godly sportsman'.

ABOVE The Pink Bedroom, with Chippendale four-posters and tapestries with scenes from *Don Quixote*, attributed to James Bridges of Hatton Garden *circa* 1680.

of Napoleon's bungled expeditionary force at Fishguard in 1797) first built a sturdy factor's house on the south (overlooking Sir Archibald's garden) which was subsequently extended and grafted on to the castle itself. Then, in 1855, Sir Hugh's leaky library roof was replaced with a pitched roof containing pedimented dormers. A balancing wing was done in the same style and on the east the flourish of a corbelled hanging turret was added to the composition.

These 19th-century improvements were attractively in keeping, right down to the engaging half-moon seats at the drawbridge. Indeed today's visitor would be hard-pressed to distinguish between the authentic old castle and the Victorian touches. A tour takes in the Drawing Room (formerly the Old Hall), with its striking oil sketch of the 1st Earl Cawdor by Sir Thomas Lawrence and a full-length portrait of his father by Sir Joshua Reynolds; the Dining Room, with its oddly primitive late 17th-century fireplace; the pretty Pink Room and the Tapestry Room, with its four-poster and Italian Baroque bedhead. The collection of tapestries at Cawdor is outstanding – ranging from late 17th-century Arras in the Tapestry Room depicting the Story of Noah to the slightly later Adventures of Don Quixote (of mysterious, possibly Soho, provenance) in the Dining Room.

Brussels tapestries adorn the Tower Room, where the pictures on display are characteristically eclectic – echoing Jacob Bogdoni's study of a magpie to be found here. An early Claude landscape hangs harmoniously with works by artists as varied as Stanley Spencer, John Piper and Carel Weight, as well as cartoons by Charles Addams and Salvador Dali (of Macbeth, who else?). Masterpieces sit happily beside mementoes in a gloriously unmuseum-like manner.

Family portraits are brought to invigorating life by the sparklingly irreverent descriptions in the guide-book, and in the room captions, by Hugh, the mercurial 6th Earl Cawdor who died in 1993, aged only 60. He summed up his family's history as 'good plain cooking with an occasional pinch of red pepper', though his great friend Sir Iain Moncreiffe of that Ilk, Bt, would point out that the courageous Campbells of Cawdor, drawn from only about 50 male descendants, had notched up no less than three VCs and 16 DSOs, as well as numerous other orders and decorations for gallantry in the last century or so. 'It would be amazing,' claimed Sir Iain, 'if anything approaching these figures for steadfast gallantry ever applied to the first 50 people stopped in any street in Britain.' Typically, Hugh Cawdor countered this stirring sentiment by quoting a tetchy friend's reaction to Sir Iain's paean: 'Yes, but suppose they were 50 young women all pushing prams as a result of all that gallantry.'

Cawdor Castle remains the cherished family home of the 6th Earl's widow, the former Countess Angelika Lazansky von Bukowa. From the tips of the turrets to the impenetrable depths of the lower garden maze beside the ambrosial mimosa, this enchanting place is still essentially very much what the 17th Thane of Cawdor described in the 18th century: an 'ancient, honourable and agreeable seat'.

Detail of Drawing Room chimneypiece of 1684 showing the heraldic emblems of the Calder family ('Calder' being an old spelling of Cawdor): the hart's head and the buckle.

LEFT Staircase landing, with tartan carpet of the sett accepted officially as 'Campbell of Cawdor' in the 1880s – when, according to the 25th Thane, 'it became fashionable to fuss furiously about distinct clan tartans'.

RIGHT 'Mind your head', goes one of the 25th Thane's injunctions in the castle guidebook, 'unless you are a Papuan pygmy'.

5

DUNROBIN CASTLE

SUTHERLAND

Y OU have to go a long way north to see Dunrobin Castle – it is by far the most northerly of Scotland's great houses – but the journey is abundantly worthwhile. For there can be few more amazing sights in the British Isles than the view from the sea beyond Golspie, taking in the majestic formal gardens and the terraces leading up to the fairytale palace perched on the cliff. The gloriously dotty skyline puts one in mind of 'mad' King Ludwig of Bavaria, or even Disneyland.

Yet buried underneath the 19th-century French Renaissance flourishes of Sir Charles Barry for the 2nd Duke of Sutherland is a venerable Scottish seat with the proud claim of being one of Britain's oldest continuously inhabited houses. Certainly the Earldom of Sutherland is one of Scotland's most ancient titles, dating back to about 1235. The Scottish kings who regained Sutherland from the Norsemen in the 12th century conferred the vast territory to Hugh, Lord of Duffus, whose son, William, was created Earl of Sutherland by King Alexander II.

Dunrobin (the name is thought to mean 'Robin's Castle' after Robert, the 6th Earl of Sutherland, son-in-law of the barbarous 'Wolf of Badenoch') is mentioned in a document for the first time in 1401 as a stronghold of the family, though the core of the present building may well be older than that. Christopher Hussey, in his classic study of *The Work of Sir Robert Lorimer* (the architect described as the 'Scots Lutyens', who remodelled the interior of the castle after it was gutted by fire during the First World War), considered there was 'little doubt that the keep was originally built about 1275'. The quadrangle came into being later, and the whole was apparently 're-edified and built againe' during the reign of King Charles II, as well as being done over in the 18th century. The old harled house – which still stands, forming the west wing – appears to have had pointed towers and a row of battlements (removed during the 19th-century alterations) round the parapets.

The succession to the Earldom of Sutherland, which can pass through the female line in default of male heirs, has been the cause of considerable friction down the centuries. In the early 16th century Alexander Sutherland, a bastard (or, as he claimed, legitimate) son of the erratic 8th Earl, made a thorough nuisance of himself. He opposed the succession first of John (the 9th Earl, who inherited his father's incapacity) and then of his sister, Elizabeth Gordon. A series of protracted lawsuits ensued and, according to Aeneas Mackay's preface to the *Exchange Rolls* of the time, Adam Gordon (Elizabeth's husband) 'used the machinery of the law and the great influence of the Huntly family... to oust the claims both of John and Alexander Sutherland, by treating the former as an idiot and the latter as a bastard'. The saga, however, did not confine itself to the law courts: twice Alexander managed to seize and occupy the castle. He was imprisoned in Edinburgh for his pains before being killed in a skirmish in 1520. Sir Robert Gordon's *Genealogical History of the Earldom of Sutherland* records that 'His head was careid to Dounrobin on a spear, and was placed vpon the height of the great tour'.

ABOVE The Gallery, with billiard table, leading out to the Great Staircase.

PRECEDING PAGES View up to the terraces and the turreted ducal palace from the gardens.

RIGHT The Drawing Room: created by Sir Robert Lorimer after the 1915 fire by throwing together two smaller rooms. The lace-like armorial ceiling, designed by Lorimer, was made by Sam Wilson in 1919. The furniture is mainly of the Louis XV period; the tapestries are Mortlake, depicting scenes from the life of Diogenes; and of the two Venetian views over the fireplaces, one is attributed to the Russian topographical master, Peter Aleksayev.

ABOVE The Queen's Corridor, named in honour of Queen Victoria, who came to stay at Dunrobin in 1872.

Then, in 1567, Elizabeth's grandson, 'Good Earl John', was poisoned together with his Countess at Dunrobin by an aunt supposedly bent on securing the Earldom and the estates for her son. Aunt Isabel herself blamed the evil influence of her cousin, the Earl of Caithness; 'even at her last gasp', we learn, she was still 'cursing him'.

Almost two centuries later the Earldom of Sutherland again passed to a woman amid legal controversy. The long-drawn out 'Sutherland Peerage Case', an immensely costly affair, became a *cause célèbre*. Judgment was eventually given by the House of Lords in favour of another Elizabeth, the young daughter of the 18th Earl (whose own father had narrowly avoided capture by the Jacobites when they briefly occupied Dunrobin in 1745).

The long reign of this Elizabeth – a beauty with what Byron called 'princessly manners', who was a watercolourist and correspondent of Sir Walter Scott – at Dunrobin effectively spanned the old world and the new. By the time of her death in 1839 both the castle and its enormous estates had been radically changed.

Indeed, particularly as far as the estates are concerned, 'radically' is the *mot juste*. For the notorious 'Highland Clearances' carried out on the Sutherland estates in the early 19th century in order to make larger and more up-to-date agricultural holdings, and introduce sheep, were actually inspired by progressive economic theories and reforming zeal. The irony was that Elizabeth's husband, the 1st Duke of Sutherland, who became the bogeyman of radical

demonology, was himself a liberal of advanced views. 'Like so many reformers,' as Sir Iain Moncreiffe of that Ilk, Bt, pointed out, 'he was willing to dedicate his life and fortune to making other folk do something they found desperately disagreeable for the sake of what he believed to be their future good.'

Shocked by the primitive conditions of his wife's tenantry, the Duke (originally an Englishman called George Granville Leveson-Gower, who succeeded to his father's Marquessate of Stafford and was described by the diarist Charles Greville as 'a leviathan of wealth') consulted James Loch, MP, a theorist in political economy from Edinburgh concerning 'improvements'. The results, carried out with the harshness of those days by the Duke's agents, caused terrible sufferings: 5,000 people were evicted from the glens of Sutherland. A native culture was virtually destroyed by 'progress'.

A giant statue of the 1st Duke by Sir Francis Chantrey on a mountainside outside Golspie dominates the landscape and a few agitators claim to be so upset by his looming presence that they want it pulled down. History, however, cannot be rewritten. If nothing else, the statue serves as a reminder of the dangers of do-goodery.

Lorimer's charming sycamore-lined Library, dominated by Philip de Laszlo's romantic portrait of the wife of the 5th Duke of Sutherland. Notwithstanding her somewhat skimpy attire in this chiffony study, Duchess Eileen served as Mistress of the Robes to Queen Mary.

The Green and Gold Room, done up in the French style for Duchess Eileen in 1921. The gilt four-poster (formerly in a room which is now part of the Library) was slept in by Queen Victoria on her visit to Dunrobin in 1872.

The 2nd Duke of Sutherland left a more universally admired memorial in the fantastic shape of the castle itself. Shortly after he succeeded to the Dukedom in 1833 he commissioned Sir Charles Barry (celebrated as the architect of the Houses of Parliament) to transform a traditional Scottish castle into a Franco–Scots extravaganza. Barry's ambitious plans took the shape of a vast triangle of buildings, with the east side of the old castle as its base, designed in a French Renaissance version of the original style, complete with dormers and steep conical roofs. The yellow sandstone used in the building operations by W. Leslie of Aberdeen (who slightly modified some of Barry's wilder fancies in the execution) even bears a resemblance to that used on the *châteaux* of the Loire. Here is the 'Auld Alliance' with a vengeance.

Inside, the sensational staircase was constructed of Caen stone (too soft for external use), brought over from France. When Barry himself – who also rebuilt the Duke of Sutherland's other seats at Trentham in Staffordshire and Cliveden on the Thames – came north to inspect his creation at Dunrobin in 1848 he added the imposing entrance tower as well as designing the gardens.

Unfortunately, much of Barry's work was destroyed by a fire in 1915, when the castle was being used as an auxiliary Naval hospital. Nonetheless, this has not turned out to be such a disaster as was first thought, for the architect brought in by the 5th Duke of Sutherland once the war was over, Sir Robert Lorimer, is increasingly being appreciated as one of Scotland's most accomplished and sympathetic designers. His sensitive treatment of Dunrobin's spirit has created interiors of singular charm.

Lorimer simplified and recapped Barry's entrance tower and ingeniously replanned the building inside. Two drawing rooms were knocked into one spacious, light chamber reminiscent of a long gallery. This helps show off two magnificent Venetian paintings, one of which is by the Russian topographical master Peter Aleksayev, and a set of four Mortlake *Diogenes* tapestries woven after the engravings of Salvator Rosa. A lace-like ceiling completes a very pleasing composition.

There is another enriched ceiling in the Dining Room, though the Pompeian-style frieze contrasts a little jarringly with the essentially 'home-spun' atmosphere generated by the Scotch oak panelling. Lorimer's engaging fondness for native timbers is shown to especially good effect in the sycamore-finished Library. Whereas the Dining Room is dominated by Sir Thomas Lawrence's picture of Duchess Harriet (wife of the 2nd Duke and Mistress of the Robes to Queen Victoria) and her daughter, the future Duchess of Argyll, the Library is under the sway of a romantic outdoor study of Duchess Eileen (the 5th Duke's wife and Mistress of the Robes to Queen Mary) by Philip de Laszlo. Duchess Eileen had leanings to the French taste in keeping with Dunrobin's style and she was responsible for the sumptuous Green and Gold Room.

On the death of the 5th Duke in 1963 the Dukedom of Sutherland passed to the 5th Earl of Ellesmere (a descendant of the second son of the 1st Duke of Sutherland) but the Earldom of Sutherland carried on in the female line, being inherited, together with Dunrobin and its estates, by yet another Elizabeth, the present Countess. Lady Sutherland kept the castle going as a school for a time, and today her elder son, Lord Strathnaver, lives nearby with his young family and opens it to the public.

No visit to Dunrobin would be complete without calling in on the Museum in the grounds. Originally a large summerhouse, built in 1732 for the 16th Earl of Sutherland, it was turned into a museum in 1878 by the 3rd Duke of Sutherland. The 4th Duke and his wife, Duchess Millicent, a magpie-style collector, added what could be described as the 'beachcomber' elements. 'Meddlesome Millie', as she was unkindly nicknamed in the Potteries of England (where Arnold Bennett immortalized her as 'the Countess of Chell' in *The Card*) on account of her philanthropy – infinitely more successful than the 1st Duke's efforts in that direction – collected anything from a Moroccan saddle-bag to a set of Eskimo fishing-gear. These and multifarious other objects take their place in the cornucopia of curiosities beside an almost incredible mixture of Pictish stones, birds' eggs, fossils, a slipper belonging to Garibaldi, Queen Victoria's handkerchief, a tawse (intriguingly 'found on the *roof* of old Tongue Free Church School') and every conceivable type of animal – from a turtle, kudu and nylghau to a horned frog and a fox shark. Giraffes' heads jostle with elephants' trunks and rhinoceroses' tails from the bags of the 5th Duke of Sutherland, a big-game enthusiast.

In short, it is surely the most remarkable personal museum in the British Isles. Wildly 'politically incorrect', it happily survives to illustrate the unfashionable truth that private ownership brings history to life far more vividly than any State organization can ever hope to achieve, and in doing so links the past to the present and future.

ABOVE The ubiquitous wild cat of Catland, the Sutherland crest and badge. 'Catland' was the ancient Pictish province which included Sutherland and Caithness.

LEFT Big Game Golgotha: animal trophies in the astonishing Museum.

RIGHT Northern light: seascape from Castle roof.

6

TRAQUAIR HOUSE

T RAQUAIR, tucked away in the lush Tweed valley near the village of Innerleithen, is advertised in the tourist brochures as 'The Oldest Inhabited House in Scotland'. Such claims are frequently made – indeed the previous chapter, on Dunrobin, mentioned one – and difficult to establish, but in this case one is happy to accept it, along with the stirring family tradition of the Bear Gates ('the Steekit Yetts'), which were closed after Bonnie Prince Charlie's departure, never to be opened again until a Stuart King is restored to the throne. For so overwhelming is the romance of this enchanting, quintessentially Scottish seat of a nobly Catholic and Jacobite dynasty that conventional critical faculties are melted away.

The precise historical facts about Traquair – and there is a mine of material contained in the family papers – seem to matter much less than its extraordinarily eloquent spirit. Catherine Maxwell Stuart, who lives there with her widowed mother, Flora, the owner of the estate, expresses this point nicely when, recalling how much her father told her about Traquair's history, she says, 'Most of all I think I learnt from him to appreciate the wonderful atmosphere.' There is indeed, as she puts it, 'a tranquillity and peace that is hard to find nowadays'.

No writer has come closer to defining Traquair's very special character than the peerless architectural historian Mark Girouard. There is something, he observed, about the proportions of the rooms, with their painted panelling, which makes them intimate and full of charm: 'One gets a vivid impression in walking through them of courteous, old-fashioned people who were prepared to suffer for their ideals, who never had much money but who had an eye for making their rooms attractive and a little unusual.'

Above all, Traquair is a refreshingly friendly, unstuffy and welcoming place. Whether you are studying the evocative Stuart relics (such as Mary Queen of Scots's rosary, crucifix, purse and the silk bedcover which she worked), worshipping in the Chapel (with its moving First World War memorials), supping the potent Traquair Ale (brewed by the traditional process in old vats) in the tea room, or blundering about in the ingenious new maze at the back of the house, you somehow feel at home.

The documents on display in the Museum Room help to bring Traquair's history to life. Originally a hunting lodge of the Scottish Kings, it received its first recorded royal visit in 1107, from King Alexander I, who granted a charter from Traquair. Later in the century William 'the Lion', who is said to have regarded Traquair as his favourite residence, signed here the charter authorizing the establishment of 'Bishop's Burgh' on the banks of the Molendinar – which was to grow into the city of Glasgow.

As you look at the main front of the house today – solid, harled, dormered and steeply pitched – it is not immediately apparent which generation was responsible for which bit of building. As Mark Girouard has written, 'It grew bit by bit, a little on top and a little on one side, so gently and all of a piece.' The oldest part of the house, to the left, has the remains of a Pele tower with narrow newel staircase.

Situated on a bend of the River Tweed, Traquair would have occupied a strong strategic position during the years of Border warfare. Two less welcome royal visitors were the English Kings Edwards I and II when the house was occupied by English troops. Eventually, after numerous changes of ownership, Traquair was granted, in 1469 by the artistic and morose King James III to his current favourite, William Rogers, described as 'Master of Music'.

Then, nine years later, a curious transaction took place, as recorded in the Museum Room. Rogers sold Traquair and all its lands to the King's uncle, 'Hearty James', Earl of Buchan, for the paltry sum of 70 Scots merks (£3.15s.10d) – to be paid in two instalments. Peter Maxwell Stuart, 20th Laird of Traquair, described this in his history of the house, as 'one of the most remarkable deeds of sale in history'. Presumably the document was drawn up under duress, for when Hearty James's far from hearty nephew King James III was absent abroad in 1482, Hearty James and his cronies lost no time in stringing Rogers up from Lauder Bridge.

Hearty James had his eye on Traquair as a handy property for his second son, James Stuart, who duly became the 1st Laird of the present line of owners. The charter of 1491 confirming him in possession describes the 'turris et fortalicis de Trakware'. In other words, a freestanding tower rising to a height of three storeys and an attic with walls varying in thickness from 4 feet 9 inches to 6 feet 9 inches. James's plans to extend the building came to nought when he was killed at the Battle of Flodden.

His son William, the 2nd Laird, made various additions; for example, the remarkably early mural painting in the Museum Room, which shows birds, beasts and vines bordered by scriptural texts, probably dates from his time, *circa* 1530. This was discovered at the beginning of the 20th century under a covering of wallpaper.

The 4th Laird, John Stuart, was knighted by Mary Queen of Scots, who appointed him Captain of the Queen's Guard. Following the murder of her musician and favourite, David Rizzio, he organized her midnight escape from Holyrood to Dunbar. Shortly afterwards Mary and her husband Lord Darnley came to stay at Traquair for a hunting expedition. The Laird was unimpressed by Darnley's coarse manners and had the courage to rebuke him over dinner when he referred to the Queen as 'a mare'. As her secretary recorded, Darnley was told in no uncertain terms that he did not speak 'like a Christian'.

The next Laird, Sir William Stuart, a courtier of King James VI, left his initials on a window lintel on the west front of Traquair, commemorating the building improvements carried out in 1599. More substantial alterations were

PRECEDING PAGES The Bear Gates ('Steekit Yetts'), built in 1737–8 for the 4th Earl of Traquair, and closed after Bonnie Prince Charlie's visit in 1745 – never to be opened again until a Stuart King is crowned in London.

RIGHT Staircase landing.

BELOW The main stairs, and a carved oak door (brought from Terregles House, Dumfriesshire) of 1601, showing two animals locked in combat – the Scottish unicorn and the English lion.

ABOVE Library catalogue: the collection of about 3,000 books has remained almost intact since the collection was first formed in the early-18th century.

LEFT The Library, restored to its original 18th-century appearance. The portraits of the philosophers and writers around the ceiling are a device for cataloguing the books.

made during the time of the 7th Laird, who was created Earl of Traquair in 1633 by King Charles I. The new young Lord Traquair rose rapidly to become Lord High Treasurer of Scotland and the most powerful man in Scotland after the King, but he became spectacularly unstuck amid the fierce religious differences of that turbulent period. His fall in 1641 and confinement to his estates, however, were to have a beneficial effect on Traquair itself.

Besides changing the course of the Tweed away from the house, he added an extra storey and, by regularizing – to a degree – the fenestration, left the main part of the building looking very much as it does today. Almost the only decorative feature outside is the series of pedimented dormer windows in the steep roof and the little corner turrets, which both reflect the French influence.

Initially Lord Traquair played no significant part in the Civil War and his role in the Battle of Philiphaugh in 1645 remains the subject of controversy. Having sent a troop of horse under his son, Lord Linton, to join his kinsman the Marquess of Montrose, he then withdrew them on the night before the battle, prompting mutterings about treachery – if not from Montrose himself, who subsequently called at Traquair for shelter during his retreat. This shelter, though, was denied him: the great door remained firmly locked and bolted.

ABOVE Part of a mural painting in the Museum Room discovered in 1900 under wallpaper. It dates from 1530 and is one of the earliest of its kind to be found in Scotland. Above and below the hound are quotations from the Acts of the Apostles.

RIGHT Still going strong: Traquair's ales.

The next year Lord Traquair re-entered public life in support of the ill-fated Charles I only to suffer another dramatic reverse when he was taken prisoner by the Cromwellians at the Battle of Preston in 1648. There followed four years of imprisonment in England, at Warwick Castle, and then a tragic decline. Stories were told of him begging in the streets of Edinburgh ('in antick garb'); it was said that he 'wanted bread before he died' and that 'he had nought to pay for cobbling his boots'.

After the death in 1659 of 'the Beggar Earl', Traquair became a bastion of Catholicism when his son, the 2nd Earl, embraced the Old Faith. He married two Catholic wives in succession, and the concealed staircase (at the back of a cupboard in the room at the top of the house where Mass was celebrated) probably dates from the time of the second wife, Lady Anne Seton. It provided a quick escape route for priests during the Penal era when the house was searched. In 1688, the year of the so-called 'Glorious Revolution', a Presbyterian mob from Peebles ransacked Traquair and destroyed all the 'Popish Trinkets' they could find.

Traquair also became a stronghold of Jacobitism as well as of Catholicism. The 4th Earl was imprisoned in Edinburgh Castle at the time of the 1715 Rising. His Countess, the beautiful daughter of the 4th Earl of Nithsdale, fully shared his commitment to the cause. The present châtelaine of Traquair, Flora Maxwell Stuart, paints a vivid picture of the perils of such loyalty in her book *Lady Nithsdale and the Jacobites*, which tells of how Lady Traquair's sister-in-law courageously rescued her husband from the Tower of London. The story is enriched by the detailed letters Lady Nithsdale sent to Lady Traquair. The Dining Room at Traquair contains portraits of Lord and Lady Nithsdale, and a copy of the speech Lord Nithsdale intended to make from the scaffold.

The Dining Room is housed in one of the wings which the 4th Earl had built, or at least rebuilt, at the end of the 17th century. The two wings and the wrought-iron railings brought about the composition of a forecourt which gave an air

of formality to Traquair's entrance front. This was enhanced by the long avenue the 4th Earl planted. At the back he added a terrace, ending in two little domed pavilions, and created a formal garden, where the maze now stands.

The 4th Earl would like to have achieved even more improvements, and consulted the fashionable Edinburgh architect James Smith, but – undoubtedly for the best – the plans to rebuild much of the entrance front to make it symmetrical proved too expensive. Indeed the family's comparative poverty on account of their steadfast devotion to Catholicism and Jacobitism only helped to preserve Traquair's timeless quality.

The 5th Earl, though, managed to tickle up the interior after his release from the Tower of London, where he was sentenced to two years for his part in the 1745 Rising. Local artists were brought in to paint the panels over the doors and fireplaces. The Drawing Room features ships in harbour framed by pretty Rococo scrolls painted in gold over the fireplace, with gilded trophies of fruit and arms over the doorways. The cove in the Library – a most covetable sanctuary – is painted in *grisaille* with heads of classical writers and philosophers that are used as a means of cataloguing the books.

It was in the 5th Earl's time that Bonnie Prince Charlie is supposed to have come to stay at Traquair. As the 5th Earl bade his rightful sovereign farewell that late autumn day in 1745, so the story goes, he closed the Bear Gates (built by the 4th Earl in 1737–8) behind him and vowed that they would never be opened again until a Stuart King was crowned in London. They remain closed to this day.

The Earldom of Traquair expired in 1861 with the death of the 8th Earl, an engagingly eccentric bachelor whose passions were sharpening razors and hunting wasps (local lads were enlisted in the regimented destruction of these hated insects). He became so fed up with his family's efforts at matchmaking that he deterred potential brides by placing stinging nettles in their beds.

The King's Room, in the core of the original part of Traquair, where Mary Queen of Scots stayed in 1566. The State Bed, remodelled in the 18th century, was brought from Terregles House, home of the Maxwell family. The hand-stitched silk quilt is said to have been worked by the Queen and her 'Four Maries' (ladies-in-waiting).

Traquair: quintessentially Scottish.

The estate, which the 8th and last Earl had economically reduced and modernized, passed to his redoubtable spinster sister, Lady Louise Stuart, who lived to nearly 100. Next, Traquair was inherited by her kinsman Henry Constable Maxwell (who duly took the surname of Stuart), brother of the 10th Lord Herries and a descendant of the Jacobite Earl of Nithsdale as well as of the 4th Earl of Traquair.

Freed from anti-Catholic restrictions, the family resumed service to their country: no less than four Maxwell Stuart boys were killed in action or died of wounds between 1916 and 1918, as recorded in the Chapel (converted from an old storeroom above the Brew House). The Brew House itself was revived by Peter Maxwell Stuart, the 20th Laird, and continues to thrive as the demand for traditional 'real ales' grows ever stronger.

Peter's parents, who came to live at Traquair during the Second World War following the deaths of two bachelor Lairds, did much to restore the place and to bring it, sympathetically, into the modern world (electricity was eventually installed in the 1950s). They opened Traquair to the public and Peter, in turn, dedicated himself to its development and preservation until his death in 1990.

His widow and daughter, both accomplished businesswomen as well as students of history, carry on the good work. For all the peace and serenity, Traquair buzzes with life. Not for nothing did the great chronicler of Borders life, Sir Walter Scott, find inspiration for the 'House of Tullyveolan', the 'Bears of Bradwarline' and 'Shaw's Castle' in this supremely Scottish shrine of the Stuarts.

7

THIRLESTANE CASTLE

BESIDES being a thrilling piece of architecture – a huge sandstone castle built on a 'T'-plan with an ingenious cluster of turrets and pinnacles – Thirlestane, set in wooded parkland above the Border town of Lauder, has a special significance for everyone interested in heritage matters. For its ownership has set an encouraging precedent for the survival of such places as family homes rather than as bureaucratically-run museums.

In 1984 Captain Gerald ('Bunny') Maitland-Carew, who had inherited Thirlestane Castle a dozen years earlier from his maternal grandmother, the Countess of Lauderdale (widow of the 15th Earl), gave the main part of this great building, together with its contents, to a charitable trust set up for its preservation, which was then endowed by the National Heritage Memorial Fund. This innovative partnership between the public and private sector – creating, in effect, a sort of 'mini National Trust' – came to be known as the 'Thirlestane Formula'. It has since been put into practice at several other historic houses, including Paxton, also in Berwickshire, and seems set to provide an invigorating alternative to the often prohibitively expensive 'safety nets' of the official National Trusts for troubled family seats.

The trouble with Thirlestane when Bunny Maitland-Carew and his wife Rosalind came to live at the castle in 1972 was basically dry rot. They were faced with a rescue operation on a colossal scale. No fewer than 40 serious outbreaks of dry rot demanded attention and the massive central tower (added for the 9th Earl of Lauderdale by David Bryce in 1840) was leaning alarmingly backwards. With the help of grants from the Historic Buildings Council a phenomenal programme of work was carried out: new steel support beams were installed, the stonework was extensively rebuilt, timbers replaced, the famously ornate drawing-room ceilings repaired, the principal rooms completely redecorated.

Yet there still remained much to be done, as indeed there always would, and prospects for the future of Thirlestane looked bleak with no means of

PRECEDING PAGES The Entrance Front, with its grand staircase.

LEFT and BELOW Details of George Dunsterfield's plasterwork, notable for its deep relief. He worked at the castle from 1674 to 1676 and is thought to have been inspired by the Italian Renaissance artist Andrea Mantegna.

RIGHT Looking through from the Ante-Drawing Room to the Long Drawing Room. The swan-pedimented doorcases in the Ante-Drawing Room recall those supplied by the joiner Thomas Carter at Ham House in Surrey in 1639; Sir William Bruce is known to have used two German craftsmen who had worked at Ham to carry out this joinery, which evokes the fantastic palaces found east of the Rhine.

funding the maintenance of the castle. Hence Bunny Maitland-Carew's negotiations with the National Heritage Memorial Fund, which endowed the charitable trust with a cash sum to allow for its continuing management and maintenance.

On show in the castle is a display recording the detail of the rescue operation, with some instructive, not to say startling, 'before' and 'after' photographs. The exhibition also helps to clarify Thirlestane's complex architectural history. Essentially, what we see today is the result of three periods of building: the 1590s, the 1670s and the 1840s.

The first stage was the responsibility of John Maitland, Lord Chancellor of Scotland and the 1st Lord Maitland of Thirlestane. His elder brother, William, celebrated as Mary Queen of Scots's Secretary of State, had inherited the principal family seat of Lethington Castle (now called Lennoxlove, and the home of the Dukes of Hamilton) in East Lothian, but John, having established himself in his own right, determined to build a pile befitting his powerful status. According to the diarist John Melvill, Chancellor Maitland was 'a man of grait learning, wisdome and stoutness…and, indeid…a grait instrument in keiping the King af the Kirk, and fra faworing of the Papists'.

The Thirlestane estate had been in the Maitland family since the mid-13th century when Sir Richard Maitland married Avicia, daughter and heiress of Thomas du Thirlestane. With its prominent position overlooking Leader Water some 28 miles south-east of Edinburgh, Thirlestane was strategically placed to defend the city from the south. A large Border fort, built in the 13th century, occupied the site chosen by Chancellor Maitland for his new keep. The keep forms the stem of the 'T'-shape of Thirlestane, and was at the time of its construction in the 1590s considered remarkable for its symmetry, with four large corner towers along its flanks.

The second stage in the building of Thirlestane came about on the creation of the 2nd Earl of Lauderdale (the Chancellor's grandson) as Duke of Lauderdale in 1672. A highly colourful and controversial character, the Duke is known to history as the 'L' in King Charles II's 'Cabal' administration. His estates had been sequestrated by the Cromwellians after he was taken prisoner at the Battle of Worcester in 1651 and he languished for nine years in the

Tower of London, but he bounced back at the Restoration of Charles II, who made him his Secretary of State for Scotland. As virtually the uncrowned 'King of Scotland' Lauderdale wielded enormous power, especially following his second marriage to the haughty heiress of Ham House in Surrey, the Countess of Dysart, when he was granted a dukedom. He decided to make a sensational splash at Thirlestane.

Inside, the Duke ordered the State Rooms to be of as 'fine worke as possible'. The English plasterer George Dunsterfield obliged with an amazing series of immensely rich and elaborate ceilings. The gloriously lush and robust plasterwork, bursting with the confident exuberance of the Carolean Age, is undoubtedly the highlight of a visit to Thirlestane. There are particularly juicy examples in the three Drawing Rooms, adorned with garlands of flowers, leaves, grapes and the Lauderdale heraldic eagles.

The Duke's architect for the lavish remodelling was Sir William Bruce, master of the Scottish Renaissance. Bruce's satisfying sense of 'mass' in a building is splendidly exemplified at Thirlestane. His genius enabled the palace that the irrepressible Duke craved to retain the feeling of a castle. He planned the construction

LEFT The ubiquitous Lauderdale eagle (which supports the Maitland coat-of-arms) nestling at the foot of an elaborate gilded drawing-room mirror.

ABOVE   The Dining Room, in the south wing added by William Burn and David
Bryce in the 1840s. The Jacobean-style ceiling is by James Annan and is thought
to have been based largely on the oldest surviving ceiling in the house of *circa*
1590. The dining chairs were made for the Duchess of Richmond's Ball on the eve
of Waterloo. Taking pride of place among the fine collection of family portraits is,
of course, the Duke of Lauderdale, looking suitably florid above the fireplace.

of the two new front towers and the grand staircase, which together dominate the approach to the castle.

The dramatic composition of the entrance reflects the Restoration love of spectacle and pomp. No one could ride up to the front door; all had to dismount at the foot of the broad flight of steps before the grand terrace. Under Bruce, the King's mason Robert Mylne worked on the house, and the Duke's apartments were embellished by Dutch craftsmen and German joiners.

All this grandeur appears to have gone to the Duke's already large head. He has certainly received a mixed press from his contemporaries and from historians. Lord Clarendon observed that Lauderdale was 'insolent, imperious, flattering and dissembling, and having no impediment of honour to restrain him from doing anything that might satisfy any of his passions'. Lord Macaulay judged him 'loud and coarse both in mirth and anger...under the outward show of boisterous frankness the most dishonest man in the whole Cabal'. Perhaps the fairest verdict was delivered by Sir Henry Craik:

> To natural talent he added a scholarship and linguistic acquirements [for example, he spoke fluent Hebrew] which were rare in his age. Intellectually he towered above his contemporaries. Creeds and principles for which his countrymen were ready to do battle or die, were for him mere playthings in the game of intrigue.

BELOW The restoration work goes on: clutter in an upper room at Thirlestane.

ABOVE Classical figure on the crouch in the Large Drawing Room.

BELOW The front door: the stone surround designed by Sir William Bruce in the 1670s contains the intertwined initials of his client, the Duke of Lauderdale, and his wife, who was the Countess of Dysart in her own right.

Yet, for all his faults, it is difficult not to warm to this larger-than-life character, memorably described by Bishop Burnet as 'very big, his hair red, hanging oddly about him; his tongue was too big for his mouth which made him bedew all that he talked to'. Greedy and crude, he was prone to gobble a leg of lamb before going out to dinner and, hardly surprisingly, was a martyr to indigestion. He would complain, in his broad Scots brogue, that the pain in his stomach was 'closer to my arse than my jewels'. At Court he joshed the Bishop of London, 'Your Grace, you're snoring so loudly that you'll wake the King.'

Eventually, though, the King was wide enough awake, under pressure from a united front of his administration, to sack the Duke from all his offices. As Vicary Gibbs notes in *The Complete Peerage*, 'Towards the end of his career his character degenerated, and from being merely unscrupulous he was guilty of active cruelty'. The Duke was retired, without a pension, and died at Tunbridge Wells in 1682.

The Dukedom of Lauderdale died with him, but the Earldom and the Thirlestane estate passed to his brother, Charles. Thirlestane ceased to be at the hub of national affairs and settled into a more domestic establishment noted for its sporting house parties.

So popular had these become by the dawn of the Victorian Age that the newly inherited 9th Earl of Lauderdale commissioned the Edinburgh architect David Bryce in 1840 to create more space at the castle. Fortunately Bryce was an admirer of Bruce's work at Thirlestane in the 1670s and his additions were broadly in sympathy with his predecessor's, though the stonework is noticeably darker than the creamy tones of the central keep.

Two large wings were built on to this keep, the south wing being constructed around a central courtyard and containing a 'Jacobean'-style dining room, new kitchens, pantries, laundries and staff bedrooms. Bryce gave the wings towers to match the outer towers of the original keep and could not resist raising the central tower which he crowned with an ogee roof flanked by a series of turrets. The result was a highly spectacular skyline.

Today the Maitland-Carews live in the north wing, and the south wing is given over to the Border Country Life Museum, an exceptionally well presented evocation of the activities on and around the country estate. The horse naturally looms large in the exhibition, for Captain Maitland-Carew, who won the Grand Military Cup at Sandown Park in 1968 and is a member of the Jockey Club, holds the Scottish Championship Horse Trials on the estate.

The old nurseries house a nostalgic collection of old toys and Captain Maitland-Carew has created a very jolly print room, in tribute to the celebrated one at his paternal home of Castletown in County Kildare. The Captain is justifiably proud of the extraordinary transformation brought about at Thirlestane. The evolution from a medieval Border fort to a 16th-century castle; from a flamboyant Baroque 17th-century palace of state and parade to a family seat and from a private estate to a public showplace has been achieved with tremendous brio. One leaves feeling all the better for the knowledge that Thirlestane's future has been secured by an imaginative scheme which should surely have far-reaching effects for the preservation of the architectural heritage.

8

SCONE
PALACE

PERTHSHIRE

T HE sacred name of Scone – albeit pronounced in several different ways – was much in the news in 1996 when the Prime Minister,
John Major, took the decision to return the legendary 'Stone of
Destiny' to Scotland exactly 700 years after it had been removed
to England by King Edward I, 'the Hammer of the Scots'. As
the Prime Minister said at the time, the Stone of Scone 'holds a
special place in the hearts of Scots'. The ancient Kings of Scotland
had been inaugurated on the Stone, which the local monks of Scone Abbey,
founded in the 12th century, liked to believe was the pillow on which the
biblical Jacob rested his head when he had his dream of angels ascending and
descending between heaven and earth.

Such magical qualities were irresistible to Edward I, who promptly had
the Stone inserted into the throne called the Confessor's Chair in the sacred
place of the English Kings at Westminster Abbey. The King's son and successor,
Edward II, was crowned sitting above the Stone, as were all English mon-
archs ever after. The shrine of Scone, though, never lost its historic significance
for the Scots; King Charles II was crowned here on New Year's Day, 1651, before
setting off for the fateful Battle of Worcester.

The Moot Hill, or 'Hill of Credulity', that rises a hundred yards north of the
present Scone Palace – seat of the Murrays, Earls of Mansfield, since 1604 – has
been aptly described as 'the heart of the Scottish Kingdom'. Made of earth from
all parts of the realm, it has witnessed the early councils of the Pictish Kings, the
embracing in the 8th century by King Nectan of 'the customs of the Church
of Rome' and possibly even the ingenious sabotaging of the Picts by Kenneth
MacAlpin in AD 835. The story goes that Kenneth, King of the Scots, while
entertaining the Pictish King Drostan and his nobles, took advantage of
'their perhaps excessive gluttony' by tipping them up inside the benches they
had imagined they had been sitting on. Caught in a trap, the Picts were
swiftly put to the sword.

After Scone became an Augustinian abbey it continued to be the fount of Scots law. Councils and Parliaments were held at Scone and the great bell would sound before the promulgation of any new law.

The Abbey came to an undignified end in the Reformation when, in 1559, a Presbyterian mob inflamed by the rantings of John Knox destroyed the place. The remnants of the ancient 'Royal City' and the monastery were given to the Ruthvens, Earls of Gowrie, who built themselves a gabled house on the ruins in about 1580. Twenty years later, though, they became unstuck through the 'Gowrie Conspiracy', a mysterious attempt to kidnap King James VI (with whom the Ruthvens had a long-running feud).

So King James decided to grant Scone to someone he could safely trust with such a precious heritage, Sir David Murray, one of his most stalwart supporters at the time of the Gowrie Conspiracy. Murray, who filled the offices of the King's Ceremonial Cup Bearer, Master of the Horse, Comptroller of Scotland and Captain of the King's Guard, was created Lord Scone in 1604.

In about 1618 Lord Scone appears to have built two principal ranges of the Palace facing south and east. The east range contained the Long Gallery, which had a painted ceiling. The picturesque gatehouse, which frames the present east front at Scone, also dates from the early 17th century.

PRECEDING PAGES The Royal Long Gallery – and it is unusually long for a Scottish house, 142 feet, in fact. As for the 'Royal' connotations, King Charles II walked down the gallery *en route* for his Coronation at Moot Hill in the grounds and Queen Victoria and Prince Albert were given a demonstration of the principles of curling on the polished floor (Scottish oak inset with bog oak). The chairs are Chinese Chippendale.

RIGHT A vaulted Gothic vestibule – one of Scone's many dramatic spaces in the interior.

BELOW The east (entrance) front framed in the arch of the early 17th-century gatehouse.

The most striking relic from this period which survives at Scone, though, is the magnificent memorial to Lord Scone, or the 1st Viscount of Stormont as he became in 1621, ten years before his death. The sumptuously carved monument in Italian alabaster was executed by Maximilian Colt (celebrated for his work at Hatfield) in 1618/19 in London and sent north. Colt charged £280 and it was money well spent.

The towering structure, one of the finest things of its kind in Scotland, shows Lord Stormont kneeling with his friends the Marquess of Tullibardine and the Earl Marischal on either side, attired in armour – and looking, as John Cornforth has nicely observed, as if they 'have stepped out of an early Inigo Jones masque'. The two friends had fallen out bitterly but their reconciliation was brought about by Lord Stormont's prayers.

It was in the time of the 3rd Viscount Stormont that King Charles II came to stay in the Palace and was crowned King of Scots on the Moot Hill – the only purely Presbyterian Coronation that has ever taken place. Unfortunately, the proceedings were rather marred by the long-windedness of the Moderator of the General Assembly of the Church of Scotland, who addressed the congregation for an hour and a half – an effort that would certainly have earned him an odds-on chance in P.G. Wodehouse's 'Great Sermon Handicap'.

ABOVE Staircase, with Murray tartan.

LEFT The Ante-Room between the Dining Room and the Drawing Room.

RIGHT The State Bed in the Ambassador's Room. The ambassador, the 2nd Earl of Mansfield, had this regal bed made out of a canopy of State which was his perquisite as King George III's Ambassador to France in the 1770s. The King's arms and cypher are liberally displayed.

There were more royal visitors in the 18th century, when the Old Chevalier and Bonnie Prince Charlie were entertained at Scone during the 1715 and 1745 Jacobite Risings respectively. Their hosts, the 5th and 6th Viscounts Stormont, were both imprisoned for their pains and had to go into exile.

A vivid picture of the character of Scone Palace in the early 18th century is given by John Loveday, the inveterate sightseer from Caversham who came here in 1732. He noted:

> The old Gate-way has CR on it : beyond ye Court that upens into, is another Court enter'd also by a Gate ... In ye 2d Court to ye left is an unroofd Row of Cloisters. The Rooms are handsome, wainscotted with Oak, & have fretwork Cielings. The Chimney-pieces are of very legant workmanship in different kinds of Marble, excellently carv'd ... The Gallery is a fine Room, has a bow'd Cieling of Wood, painted with Minitures of Stag-hunting, prospects etc. There are several Rooms within another; in one of 'em a dark Purple Velvet Bed work'd by Mary Q of Scots; in ye same Room are Needlework Hangings done by Nuns.

ABOVE and BELOW Details of Gothic carving.

Suppressing the cynical thought that 'Mary Q of Scots' must have been extremely busy with her needles – since almost every great house in Scotland offers a similar tale – it is good to report that the aforesaid embroidered velvet bed hangings are still to be seen at Scone. Among the other outstanding treasures in the Palace, hung in the present Drawing Room, is Sir Joshua Reynolds's portrait of the most eminent member of the Murray family, the 1st Earl of Mansfield, twice Lord Chief Justice and Chancellor of the Exchequer. 'Sir Joshua himself,' wrote Lord Mansfield of the portrait, 'thinks it one of the best he ever did.' In it, we see the great jurist seated and looking wonderfully wise and benign.

According to a slightly snooty account in the 1st Marquess of Lansdowne's autobiography, 'William Murray was 16 years of age when he came out of Scotland, and spoke such broad Scotch that he stands entered in the University Books at Oxford as born at Bath, the Vice-Chancellor mistaking *Bath* for Perth.' Even Lord Lansdowne had to concede, though, that he 'certainly was by nature a very eminent man, bred like all the great families of Scotland an intriguing aristocrat, poor and indefatigable, very friendly and very timid'.

'Timid' or not, 'the Silver-Tongued Murray' (as Alexander Pope dubbed him) was acclaimed for his eloquence as a lawyer and politician. Lord Chesterfield said of him, 'One might have heard a pin fall when he was speaking' in the House of Commons. He has an especially honoured place in history for his judgment in favour of a runaway Negro slave in 1771 – a decision which opened the door to the abolition of slavery, which Lord Mansfield considered 'odious'.

Although it would have been appropriate for possibly the greatest lawyer of all time to be seated in a palace steeped in the legal traditions of his native land, William was only a younger son and had to content himself with employing another great Scot, Robert Adam, to remodel his Hampstead residence, Kenwood House. Scone itself was inherited by his nephew, the 7th Viscount Stormont, a brilliant diplomatist *en poste* in Dresden, Vienna and finally Paris. In 1773 he wrote that the house 'can never be made a tolerable habitation without immense expense which it can never deserve'. Nonetheless, a few years later he brought in the Edinburgh architect George Paterson to turn the palace into what Lord Stormont (who eventually succeeded to one of his famous uncle's Earldoms of Mansfield in 1793) called 'a very convenient habitation'.

It was not, though, until the time of his son, the 3rd Earl of Mansfield that Scone acquired its present Georgian Gothic appearance. 'Almost all people have follies,' wrote this Lord Mansfield (a Fellow of the Royal Society and of the Society of Antiquaries), 'this is one which will have at least some advantage. The family had no residence and little interest anywhere. Though I shall have not ensured their interest yet I shall have given them a handsome and agreeable residence.'

In 1802, after toying with the idea of remodelling the interior in a post-Adam classical style to designs by George Saunders, the 3rd Earl commissioned the comparatively unknown William Atkinson, a pupil of James Wyatt, to construct a castellated affair in red sandstone. As the architectural historian Colin McWilliam has observed: 'Square, sober and reasonable, it has little to do with his later Abbotsford [*qv*] and the romantic baronial style.'

The rooms are ample and well-lit, with Gothic details down to the pelmets and chandeliers. The halls and Gallery are attractively vaulted or beamed in a style that is suitably monastic in reference to Scone's sacred past. The costs of the lengthy building operations certainly confirmed the fears of Lord Mansfield's father about 'immense expense'. More than £60,000 had been spent by the end of 1811.

Whatever Atkinson's architecture may lack in excitement, it serves as a fine, understated setting for a marvellously varied collection of furniture and works of art – ranging from exotic 17th-century cabinets and tables from Germany and Italy to lacquered English Regency pieces and a feast of Boulle. The

A range and copper pots in the Old Kitchen. The room is now used as a restaurant for visitors.

Drawing Room (formerly the dining room) features a set of Louis XV armchairs with strikingly bold needlework and an exquisite marquetry writing table made for Marie Antoinette by the great *ébéniste* Jean-Henri Riesener.

The present Dining Room contains a remarkable collection of continental ivories, including Augsburg Baroque, while the Royal Long Gallery – where the original 16th-century parquetry floor, inlaid with bog oak, was happily retained by Atkinson – boasts the unparalleled set of *vernis Martin* vases and

The Dining Room, with its outstanding collection of large European ivories. The Chippendale design chairs and oak tables were supplied by Ballingals of Perth. Salamon Koninck's 17th-century painting of *The Philosopher* hangs over the fireplace.

RIGHT The west front of the palace.

objets d'art mounted in silver gilt or ormolu. The technique of painting on *papier mâché* under a lacquer varnish, developed by the Martin brothers of Paris, died with them so the importance of Scone's set cannot be overestimated. The Gothic shelves of the Library are filled with porcelain – Meissen, early Sèvres, Chelsea 'red anchor' and many more delectable items.

The present arrangement of the interior owes much to the 7th Earl of Mansfield and his Countess, who courageously moved back into the Palace in the 1950s after it had been unoccupied – other than as a girls' school during the Second World War – for 30 years, and also to their son, the present Earl, and his Countess. Lady Mansfield, a former chairman of the Scottish branch of the Historic Houses Association, has enthusiastically developed the opening arrangements of the Palace (so that visitors have reached the 100,000 a season mark) and is a tireless and knowledgeable custodian of its treasures. Lord Mansfield, a former Minister of State in both the Scottish and Northern Ireland Offices and latterly first Crown Estates Commissioner, takes a special interest in the 25,000-acre estate.

Indeed, Scone was one of the first historic houses open to the public to have a room exhibiting the workings of the estate, that vital support. 'Although my home is old,' Lord Mansfield tells visitors, 'I hope you will agree that the Estate is run on thoroughly modern lines with the object of providing a secure livelihood for as many people as possible, for maintaining intact and unspoiled a piece of beautiful Scottish countryside, and with your help, to generate enough money to keep Scone as it is today in the years ahead.'

A special corner of the estate, not far from the Palace and the Abbey ruins, is the Pinetum, dominated by a vast fir. Its original seed was sent back to Scotland in 1826 by a son of Scone, the celebrated horticulturist David Douglas, who began life as an under-gardener at the Palace. His tragic end also had faint echoes of Scone – bearing in mind the trap-door banquet which undid the Picts. On one of his horticultural expeditions he fell into a pit dug by natives to catch wild bison. Unfortunately, he thereby found himself keeping close company with another occupant of the pit, a bull bison who in a most unneighbourly manner gored him to death.

9

DALMENY HOUSE

WEST LOTHIAN

I N THE HALL at Dalmeny – the first Gothic Revival house in Scotland – hangs a striking conversation piece by Carlos Sancha of the present Earl of Rosebery and his family in the sweeping parkland beside the Firth of Forth. Painted in 1978, it depicts Lady Rosebery, a former stage designer whose imaginative flair has revitalized the interior of the house, holding some of the catalogues for the celebrated Mentmore Towers sale of the previous year – a permanent reminder of the event that effectively sparked off the present 'heritage industry'.

What was not generally appreciated at the time was that Lord and Lady Rosebery, far from selling up the entire treasures at Mentmore Towers in Buckinghamshire – which came into the family through the marriage in 1878 of the 5th Earl, the Prime Minister, to Hannah, only daughter and heiress of Baron Meyer de Rothschild – were merely rationalizing and concentrating their collections. Following the death of the 6th Earl of Rosebery, a legendary figure on the Turf, in 1974, the new Earl and his wife intended to offer Mentmore and most of its contents to the Government, but when that initiative famously floundered it was resolved to take the best things up to Scotland and to sell the rest which was unsuitable for Dalmeny. And so the cream of Baron Meyer's collection of 18th-century decorative arts – tapestries, carpets, porcelain, paintings and furniture – came north. The result is that this great house only a few miles from the centre of Edinburgh houses fabulous objects of a quality quite unsurpassed in Scotland.

The Dalmeny estate has been in the family since 1662 when Sir Archibald Primrose, a lawyer who had succeeded his father as Clerk to the Privy Council and eventually became Lord Clerk Register of Scotland, bought the Barony of Barnbougle from the Hamiltons, Earls of Haddington. The original structure on the property, Barnbougle Castle, a 13th-century tower-house on the shore of the Firth of Forth, proved increasingly inconvenient as the sea battered away at the ancient walls.

PRECEDING PAGES The Staircase Hall framed in a Gothic arch. The single flight of stairs was the 4th Earl of Rosebery's choice; his architect, William Wilkins, wanted to build (and indeed actually began doing so) a double-branched stair. The portrait on the half-landing is of Lady Dorothea Primrose, daughter of the 2nd Earl of Rosebery (the 'black sheep' of the family who deserted his wife for a laundrymaid).

RIGHT The Dining Room, hung with portraits from the collection of the 5th Earl of Rosebery, the late-Victorian Prime Minister. On the far wall, to the left, is the 3rd Earl, portrayed by Sir Henry Raeburn in Thistle robes and one of his three wigs of varying lengths. To the right is Admiral Lord Rodney by Thomas Gainsborough.

BELOW Joseph Nollekens's marble bust of the 2nd Marquess of Rockingham in the Dining Room at Dalmeny. One of Lord Rosebery's predecessors as Prime Minister, the Whiggish Lord Rockingham, infuriated King George III by his support for American independence.

ABOVE Detail of the gilded bronze decoration on an early 18th-century safe (possibly by Charles Cressent) in the Drawing Room.

BELOW Detail of gilded bronze decoration on the Louis XVI upright secretaire in the Drawing Room. Designed in the workshop of J.F. Oeben, it was completed after his death, in 1763, by J.H. Riesener.

Yet Barnbougle was to remain the family seat for more than a century as the Primrose dynasty weathered various vicissitudes. In the early 1700s, Sir Archibald's son and namesake, a courtier to Queen Anne, was advanced to the Viscountcy and then the Earldom of Rosebery; but the 2nd Earl, the black sheep of the family, was imprisoned for riot and debt and largely dissipated his inheritance. He deserted his wife for a laundrymaid, and when she, in turn, left him he advertised for her to be returned, as she had taken some of his linen, 'for a two guineas reward, and no questions will be asked'.

When questions were asked by the offspring of the 3rd Earl of Rosebery about when they might have a more up-to-date home, Lord Rosebery was wont to reply – even though he had been drenched by a wave which came in through the dining-room window – 'What was good enough for my grandfather should be good enough for my grandchildren.' In his younger days, though, the 3rd Earl, fired up by his Grand Tour, had been full of enthusiasm for improving Barnbougle. He freed the estate of debt, reorganized the farming, enclosed fields and planted trees. Bolstered by the fortune of his first wife, Susan Ward, a Norfolk heiress who died childless in 1771, the 3rd Earl commissioned his friend Robert Adam to design a spectacular triangular castle, complete with harbour, incorporating the old Barnbougle tower-house. Not only was this a case of anything his near neighbours the Hopes of Hopetoun (*qv*) could do, Lord Rosebery could do better, but the rather vain Earl (who used to disguise his baldness by wearing three wigs of different lengths and would periodically set off for a 'haircut' in Edinburgh carrying the shortest hairpiece in a box) considered a spanking new pile would improve his chances of re-marriage.

Sadly, Adam's sublime fantasy never became a reality and the 3rd Earl's young bride and her brood had to withstand the rigours of old Barnbougle, patched up by a Mr Salisbury who was described by the disgruntled Earl as 'a lying, ill-tempered, vulgar builder'. The long-awaited new house had to wait until the death of the old boy, aged 86, in 1814.

The 4th Earl of Rosebery, a member of the Society of Dilettanti , had a particular interest in architecture and determined to build a completely new house on a separate site a quarter of a mile away. Before his father's death he toyed with Classical designs by William Atkinson (who remodelled Scone Palace – *qv*) and William Burn, but his careful observations in England and Wales – the Napoleonic Wars had precluded a Grand Tour – had converted his taste to Tudor Gothic.

Two architects, Jeffry Wyatt (later 'Wyatville' of Windsor Castle fame) and William Wilkins (best known for the National Gallery in London), were invited to submit designs for the new Dalmeny House. Wyatt sketched a Tudor Gothic pile, Wilkins a neo-Classical affair facing inland – away from the sea view. It seems, though, that Lord Rosebery was prejudiced in favour of Wilkins, an old Cambridge friend and fellow Dilettante, for he showed him Wyatt's design.

In any event, Wyatt was paid off and Wilkins duly produced a building which strongly recalled his and his client's East Anglian connections. Indeed the entrance front of Dalmeny is basically cribbed from the splendidly robust East Barsham Manor, near Fakenham, Norfolk, which was built for Sir Henry Fermor in about 1520. The sea facade is more symmetrical with its central tower, octagonal turrets and regular mullion and transom windows. Inside, the principal rooms are Regency in style, but the mood of the Hall (with its hammer-beam ceiling), fan-vaulted corridor and Flemish stained-glass windows in the Gallery is romantically Gothic.

Romance, however, could hardly have been on the 4th Earl's mind during the building operations when, in 1815, he was obliged to sue his brother-in-law, Sir Henry Mildmay, Bt, for 'alienating his wife's affections'. Mildmay –

RIGHT The vaulted Gothic corridor, which gives access to the State rooms.

BELOW Detail of panel of 15th-century Flemish stained glass bought by the 4th Earl of Rosebery for Bernasconi's plasterwork vault in the Gothic corridor.

ABOVE The 6th Earl of Rosebery's snug sitting room, well-stocked with masculine comfort and sporting memorabilia. Over the fireplace is a painting by Alexander Nasmyth of the 3rd Earl and his family outside Barnbougle Castle in 1784.

RIGHT The Drawing Room, featuring French furniture from the Rothschild collection formerly at Mentmore. The carpet is Savonnerie (ordered by King Louis XIV for the Louvre in 1664); the tapestries Beauvais (designed in 1740 by François Boucher in the Chinoiserie style); and the mirror above the fireplace is mid-18th-century English Rococo, also in the Chinese style. The Gothick cornice was added during the 1950s restoration of Dalmeny.

whose dead wife had been the sister of Harriet Bouverie, Countess of Rosebery – insinuated himself into Barnbougle disguised as a fisherman, having arrived at the castle from Cramond in a rowing-boat. Mud from his boots on the carpet aroused suspicion and he was discovered in Lady Rosebery's bedroom by the 4th Earl's younger brother, Frank Primrose, a barrister. Sir Henry was chased out of the window, with Lady Rosebery being sent after him by carriage the next morning. The 'guilty pair', as *The Complete Peerage* notes, were subsequently married in Stuttgart.

It was perhaps some consolation to the 4th Earl that the hefty damages he extracted from the covetous Baronet, £15,000, would have helped defray some of the costs of building Dalmeny, which amounted to £40,602. A substantial item in the accounts was the charge for Coade stone (£3,822.5s.4d) shipped up from London in the readymade form of chimneys, battlements, embrasures, turret shafts and so forth. The park was landscaped by Richard White.

In 1819, two years after its completion, J.P. Neale described the new Dalmeny House in his *Views of the Seats of Noblemen and Gentlemen* as being 'calcu-lated more for comfort and convenience than for show'. Twenty-five years later, when the young Queen Victoria visited her former bridesmaid, Lady Dalmeny (whose husband was not to succeed to the Earldom of Rosebery as, having

advocated exercise as a means to healthy living for the middle classes, he expired from pleurisy brought on by a midwinter walk back from Edinburgh's Turkish baths), she was full of praise for the comfort – and the sea view. The present Roseberys find that Wilkins's sensible adaptation of the historical style to contemporary life has enabled them to live in 'comfort and convenience' upstairs (thereby enjoying a better view of the sea) while the rest of the house has worked remarkably well for 'show'.

Today, thanks to Lady Rosebery's dramatic eye, it is undoubtedly some show. The contents have to be seen to be believed. Apart from the exquisite French 18th-century furniture, tapestries, Sèvres porcelain and paintings from Mentmore in the Drawing Room, there are early Scottish portraits of the Primroses, 17th-century Scottish furniture, Burns mementoes, Goya tapestries and, in the Dining Room, a majestic group of masterpieces by Reynolds, Gainsborough, Raeburn and Lawrence. The former billiard room is devoted to the unrivalled Napoleonic collection formed by the 5th Earl of Rosebery.

The story goes that the 5th Earl, as a boy at Eton (a school to which he was so attached that the Eton Boating Song was played, in accordance with his wishes, as he died), expressed the triple ambition – gloriously fulfilled – of becoming Prime Minister, winning the Derby and marrying a Rothschild. He collected objects and paintings not solely for their artistic merit but because

The entrance front: Tudor Perpendicular comes to Scotland by way of East Anglia (the architect William Wilkins copied much of the detail from East Barsham Manor in Norfolk). The equine statue is by Ernst Boehm of 'King Tom' (1873), the foundation stallion of Baron Meyer de Rothschild's stud. It was moved here from Mentmore in 1982.

of their connection with people he considered historically important; the Napoleonic accumulation at Dalmeny is the largest of these 'associative collections'.

Besides adorning the main house with cherished objects, the 5th Earl also rebuilt, in 1881, Barnbougle Castle, which had previously been left to the sea birds. The old place was partly demolished when explosives, stowed for quarrying, were accidentally ignited. Dalmeny itself suffered a serious fire during the Second World War after which the 6th Earl of Rosebery and his Countess brought in the architect 'Paul' Geddes Hyslop to carry out a sensitive restoration. Hyslop gave the Library a deeply coved ceiling, reused Wilkins's oak bookcases (salvaged from the flames) and installed a mid-18th-century Rococo chimney-piece (from the demolished Rosebery town house in Berkeley Square) to create a delightfully comfortable ensemble.

It was also in the aftermath of the Second World War that Dalmeny earned the right to be considered the birthplace of the Edinburgh Festival – thanks to the enterprise of the 6th Earl, chairman of the newly formed Scottish Tourist Board, and of his Countess, Eva, an accomplished amateur pianist. The present Lord and Lady Rosebery recall that during the Festival in the late Earl's time two separate groups of people would stay at Dalmeny, often without ever meeting each other:

> Lord Rosebery's shooting party left the house early after a hearty breakfast and took a picnic lunch to the grouse moors. They returned to whisky, hot baths, a large dinner and a little bridge before early bed. Lady Rosebery's Festival party (which frequently included many world-famous performers) rose late, had lunch and high tea between visits to concerts, art galleries and theatres and retired after a very late supper. It took 17 staff to keep the system running smoothly.

Dalmeny's 'double life' is nicely encapsulated in this vignette. For if a visitor is, understandably, quite overwhelmed by the sensational art-historical experience on offer in this treasure-house, he can turn with relief to the leathery masculine comfort of the 6th Earl's sitting-room – a richly atmospheric sportsman's 'den' redolent of the Turf, the chase and the cricket field. The Rosebery racing colours (rose and primrose) together with the gold, red and black of I Zingari and the chocolate of Surrey conjure up 'great days in the distance enchanted'. In his younger days, as Lord Dalmeny, the 6th Earl captained Surrey at cricket and awarded Jack Hobbs his county cap at The Oval.

The sporting colours chime with the present Countess's view of life in great houses. 'Everybody lives in, and enjoys, their own "fruit salad",' says Lady Rosebery, who opens Dalmeny to the public in the early part of the week during July and August. 'But the trouble with a "stately home" is that the bowl is too big. Each generation has to sell a few good pieces, buy some of what they personally like, and push the mother-in-law's favourites to the back. We've had to distill it, and put it into different subject areas, so it is easier to understand and enjoy.' No 'fruit salad', though, could be more sympathetically arranged or contain so many wonderfully exotic ingredients as Dalmeny.

10

KINROSS HOUSE

KINROSS-SHIRE

O N A TOUR of Scotland in 1722 Daniel Defoe, celebrated as the author of *Robinson Crusoe*, found, at the west end of Loch Leven, 'the most beautiful and regular piece of Architecture (for a private Gentleman's Seat) in all Scotland, perhaps in Great Britain'. As Defoe noted, this 'noble palace' of Kinross House had been built by 'that great architect Sir William Bruce' on an estate bought in the 'reign of King Charles II' from the Douglases, Earls of Morton. 'The House,' Defoe enthused, 'is a picture, 'tis all Beauty, the Stone is white (and fine), the Order regular, the Contrivance elegant, the Workmanship exquisite.'

A visitor today – and it should be noted that Kinross House is only open by written appointment with the present owner, Mr James Montgomery, elder son and heir of Sir David Montgomery, Bt – can do little more than echo Defoe's sentiments. For, as Sir David points out, the remarkable thing is that, during the 300 years since it was built, Kinross has not been structurally altered or significantly changed in any way. What you see is an authentic example not only of late 17th-century architecture but also of landscaping; as Defoe said, 'the great avenue from the town of Kinross is the noblest you can imagine'.

The vista does not end with the Classical symmetry of the house; it carries on through to the formal garden (magnificently re-created by Sir Basil Montgomery, 5th Bt, at the beginning of the 20th century) and thence to Loch Leven itself. Bruce ingeniously planned the axis of his house and garden to focus – through the delightful 'Fish Gate', with its cherubs and cornucopia dipping down to a basket of wriggling fish, representing the 11 species caught (at that time) in the loch – on a prospect of Lochleven Castle.

The castle was an ancient stronghold of the Douglas family (granted to them by King Robert II in 1372) and is known to history as the prison of Mary Queen of Scots from the summer of 1567 to the spring of 1568. Her gaoler, Sir William Douglas (later 5th Earl of Morton), had been implicated in the murder of Mary's

favourite, the musician David Rizzio, but Sir William's younger son, George, gallantly helped the Queen to escape by boat across the loch.

In the 17th century the Douglases, Earls of Morton, were staunch supporters of King Charles I and paid dearly for their over-generous contributions to the Royalist cause. By 1675 the 8th Earl of Morton was in such straitened circumstances that he had to sell his Kinross-shire estate to Sir William Bruce, Bt, a prosperous courtier who had played a significant role in the Restoration of King Charles II. Bruce had begun life with no great fortune, as the younger son of the Laird of Blairhall, Fife, but was well connected and had a keen eye for opportunity. His moment came when he acted as the go-between during the negotiations by General Monk, the Parliamentary Commonwealth's representative in Scotland, and the exiled King Charles in Holland. Once the Restoration came Bruce was showered with profitable offices which enabled him to acquire the Balcaskie estate in his ancestral county of Fife. As a passionate amateur of architecture and gardening, the office that would have given Bruce most satisfaction was his appointment, in 1671, as 'surveyor, contriver and overseer of all the works at the palace of Holyrood House, and of such other castles and palaces in Scotland as the King shall appoint to be repaired'.

Apart from Holyroodhouse itself, which he virtually rebuilt, Bruce's architectural talents also flourished at Thirlestane (*qv*) and Hopetoun (*qv*), but Kinross was to be his master work – not least because it has remained largely untouched. A pioneer of Palladianism in Scotland, Bruce has been hailed as Caledonia's answer to Inigo Jones and Sir Christopher Wren. Yet while Kinross fully deserves

PRECEDING PAGES The west (entrance) front from the avenue.

LEFT The east (garden) front.

RIGHT View to Loch Leven Castle from the formal gardens through the Fish Gates.

BELOW LEFT and BELOW RIGHT Details of carving around central window of west front by Dutch craftsmen.

the reputation of being Scotland's first great Classical country house, what gives the place its extraordinary charm is the hint of Scottish vernacular here and there – particularly in the Stables.

For a student of architecture Kinross's fascination is that it is *sui generis*. Mark Girouard has described it as 'a lonely masterpiece, not quite like anything that came before or after ... essentially an individual Scottish creation, a kind of sobered-up baroque palace'. One of the most intriguing aspects is why Bruce built (or attempted to build, as the interior was still incomplete when he died in 1710) such a palatial affair, worthy of comparison with the great Renaissance châteaux of France. For all his prosperity Bruce was far from a plutocrat.

Could, it has been suggested, Bruce have been intending Kinross as a residence for the Duke of York, King Charles II's unpopular brother James, in the event of his being excluded from the throne? Whatever the truth of this theory – and there is no evidence to support it – Bruce began his preparations at Kinross well before King Charles II's death. As early as 1679 he was draining, levelling, enclosing and planting the formal gardens. His son, John, was sent to France from where he brought back hundreds of seeds.

The main house appears to have been built largely between 1685 and 1691. The Cleish stone, which gives Kinross its special character, is not so much 'white', as Defoe described it, as a warm yellow streaked with reddish-brown veins. The stone is laid in massive blocks, giving the house an impressive solidity, and adorned with Corinthian pilasters and carvings round the central doors and windows.

LEFT The Drawing Room, or as Sir William Bruce called it, the Garden Hall. The overdoor paintings were supplied by Alexander Brand of Edinburgh in 1692.

RIGHT The main staircase carved from oak by (in all probability) the Dutch craftsman Jan van sant Voort, who worked with Sir William Bruce at Edinburgh's royal palace of Holyroodhouse.

An account of June 1686 records that two Dutch stone-carvers, 'Peeter Paull Boyse & Cornelius Vanerba' were paid £12 10s, though the actual signature of the receipt is by one 'Cornillis van nerven'. It is thought that the Dutchmen were mainly employed on the garlanded cartouches above the pavilion doors, the lion masks on the curving screen walls and, quite possibly, the endearing embellishments of the Fish Gate.

By this stage, the stables had been roofed but the main block had only risen as high as the basement. The summer of 1686 also marked a turning point in Sir William Bruce's career. The new Catholic King, James VII of Scotland and II of England, with whom the staunchly Episcopalian Bruce had never hit it off, sacked his brother's faithful courtier from the Privy Council.

Bruce found himself in the political wilderness, where he remained after the 'Glorious Revolution' as his Episcopalian views were viewed with equal suspicion by the new Presbyterian ascendancy under 'Dutch William'. This exile from the Court and the world of power proved a mixed blessing for Kinross. On the one hand, it meant that the building operations had Bruce's undivided attention; on the other, the source of the cash needed to decorate the interior effectively dried up.

ABOVE The Ballroom, Sir William Bruce's 'Great Sallon', which occupies most of the first floor at Kinross. Sir Basil Montgomery, 5th Bt, added the coved ceiling in the early 20th century.

RIGHT Lady Montgomery, the former Helen Graham and heiress of Kinross, by Sir Henry Raeburn in the Ballroom.

Although the entrance floor rooms were finished off much as Bruce originally intended – such as the Small Drawing Room, with its wood carving attributed to Jan van sant Voort, who worked at Holyroodhouse – the *piano nobile*, or grand suite of rooms on the first floor, remained undecorated. Indeed the present coved plaster ceiling which presides over Bruce's splendid double-height 'Great Sallon' was not inserted until the beginning of this century.

In 1775, some 50 years after Defoe's rapturous observations, Sylas Neville visited Kinross and found it 'from the negligence and indifferent circumstances of the owner [James Bruce Carstairs]... much out of repair'. Neville concluded, 'A rich Nabob might make something very magnificent here.' Sure enough, it was a Nabob, though not a very rich one, who bought Kinross a couple of years later in the person of George Graham, a merchant of Calcutta.

Graham brought in the Edinburgh architect George Paterson to re-sash the windows and make various 'improvements', none of them particularly significant. Unfortunately, though, Graham found Bruce's magnificent ornamental entrance gates too grand, and decided to tone them down.

In 1819 Graham's son, Thomas, died, leaving two daughters (the only son had been killed by pirates in the Indian Ocean) and a situation slightly reminiscent of the more or less contemporaneous scramble among the Royal Dukes to produce an heir to the throne. The Kinross estate, decreed Thomas Graham, was to be inherited by whichever of his daughters had a son who first reached 21. (At the time of his death both daughters were childless, and

ABOVE One of four original stone lion heads with iron rings used to tether horses near the front door.

LEFT Atlas in the gardens – a statue brought to Kinross in the early 1900s by Sir Basil Montgomery.

BELOW Stone lions, among the statuary introduced to the formal garden during its early 20th-century re-creation by Sir Basil Montgomery, 5th Bt.

the trustees sold up the contents of the house in a seven-day sale in the autumn of 1819.)

As the genial Sir David Montgomery relates, 'The Montgomery of the day got off the mark like a shot and married Helen Graham [Thomas's younger daughter], who gave birth to a boy six months before her less pretty sister – which, I might add, is the only reason we're here today.' Helen's beauty is strikingly captured in the full-length portrait by Sir Henry Raeburn which dominates the Ballroom (as Bruce's 'Great Sallon' was renamed).

Yet, while continuing to maintain the Kinross estate, the Montgomerys preferred to live at their ancestral home of Stobo Castle in Peeblesshire. So Kinross House slept, mercifully unspoilt, through the rest of the 19th century.

Then, in 1902, the baronetcy and the estates passed to Basil Montgomery, whose love of architecture and gardening hardly fell short of Sir William Bruce's own. Significantly his first wife was a Moncreiffe of that Ilk, whose Palladian family seat of Moncreiffe House (to be burnt with the Baronet in 1957) was, in a sense, Bruce's 'dry run' for Kinross. Determined to awake the Sleeping Beauty, Sir Basil moved into Kinross and set about restoring Bruce's masterpiece to its full glory.

The main house was sensitively repaired, with Sir Basil himself being responsible for the new ceiling in the Ballroom. He took the plasterwork over the great staircase as his model and, as Sir David comments, 'he really didn't do a bad job'. The entrance gates were reconstructed – following, as Hubert Fenwick, the admirable authority on Bruce, has suggested, the example at Melville House, Fife. Many of the family portraits were brought back (including Bruce's own) and the rooms were filled with fine furniture.

Above all, Sir Basil remade the glorious formal garden – with, as the memorial plaque in one of the pavilions at Kinross phrases it, 'timeless devotion, unerring judgment and with joy'. Today it ranks as one of the finest formal gardens in Scotland and is regularly open to the public.

11

NEWHAILES

W E WERE fortunate to visit Newhailes, an almost incredible survival of the Scottish Enlightenment now surrounded by the industrial and suburban sprawl of Musselburgh on the outskirts of Edinburgh, at a crucial moment in its history. For, in January 1997, the last private owner, Lady Antonia Dalrymple, widow of Sir Mark Dalrymple, 3rd (and last) Bt of Newhailes, was preparing to move out as the house was about to be formally handed over into the care of the National Trust for Scotland after a remarkable rescue act to save this exquisite ensemble from being dispersed.

Since Sir Mark's death in 1971, Lady Antonia had fought valiantly to preserve this 'Time Capsule' of a house in its increasingly unpromising setting, but the maintenance costs had become impossibly high. Grasping the singular importance of a place nicely described by one of its new National Trust champions as 'a battered old jewelbox, dusty and much the worse for wear – inside, to your surprise, are unique and priceless treasures', the Heritage lobby acted in unison to find the £12.7 million necessary for Newhailes's restoration and secure future. The Heritage Lottery Fund came up with £8 million; Historic Scotland granted £1.45 million for repairs; the National Art Collections Fund contributed £245,000 for the purchase of four of the outstanding portraits in the house (including two by Allan Ramsay); and the balance is being sought through public appeal by the NTS.

We were lucky enough to glimpse Newhailes in its 'Before' state – decayed, intimate, idiosyncratic to a degree, magically untouched – while scholarly and sensitive preparations were already being laid by the NTS curatorial team for the long haul to 'After'. Indeed the photographer found himself working round removal men as the contents were taken away to be put into storage so that the great programme of conservation could begin.

Much needs to be done: on closer inspection, once one has been dazzled by the beauties of Newhailes (its portraits, its ornate plasterwork, its marble chimneypieces, its needlework), you notice worrying signs of decay. There are tell-tale patches of damp, woodworm holes, cracks in frames. The NTS reckon that the delicate tasks involved will amount to the equivalent of 100,000 man hours (34 working years) in expert craftsmanship.

For a moment in time, though, we experienced Newhailes as it was – shabby and sumptuous with a compelling atmosphere which, as John Cornforth of *Country Life* (whose articles did much to focus attention on the house's plight) has pointed out, 'owes a great deal to the personality of Lady Antonia'. The photographer was privileged to capture it before the sea change.

The sea itself seems to play a significant part in the story of several great Scottish houses – unlike in England. At Newhailes one is constantly reminded of the ocean not only by its physical proximity – the vista over the Firth of Forth towards North Berwick Law is miraculously retained with the modern urban sprawl in between conveniently hidden as if by a fortuitous 'ha-ha' – but by the plethora of shells which adorn the interior. They are to be spotted in every conceivable place, even as part of the door furniture, in which tiny cockleshells hide the keyholes. And in several instances they are not imitations but genuine seashells, gilded for decoration. It is thought that this riot of shells may allude to the

PRECEDING PAGES 'The most learned room in Europe', according to Dr Johnson; the Library was once the epitome of the Scottish Enlightenment of the 18th century but is presently denuded of books. Now that Newhailes has been rescued by the nation and vested in the National Trust for Scotland, it is hoped that the National Library of Scotland will be able to return Lord Hailes's great collection.

RIGHT The portrait by Sir John Medina in the elaborate overmantel of 1742 shows Lord Hailes's father and grandfather, the 1st and 2nd Dalrymple Baronets. Sir David, the 1st Bt, began the Library; Sir James, the 2nd Bt, completed its progress into a great room.

BELOW The Winter Drawing Room, hung with family portraits by Allan Ramsay and Sir Henry Raeburn and boasting a richly carved chimney-piece by Sir Henry Cheere.

LEFT The gorgeously cluttered China Closet.

RIGHT Detail of the carving in the China Closet, off the Library. Shells are a constant *motif* in the house; some real, from the nearby shore at Musselburgh, others exuberantly created.

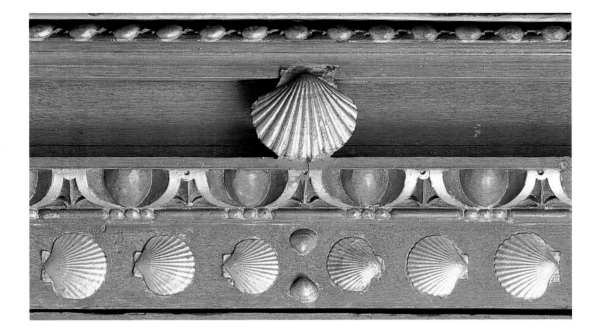

Rococo style enthusiastically adopted at Newhailes by Sir James Dalrymple, 2nd Bt of Hailes, in the 1720s and 1730s. For 'Rococo' is an Italian word derived from the French for shellwork, *rocaille*. Perhaps also Sir James, who apparently had a good sense of humour for a politician and Auditor of the Exchequer, may have intended a pun on *Mussel*burgh.

Sir James's father, Sir David Dalrymple, 1st Bt of Hailes, who was also Auditor of the Exchequer, had acquired the property, previously called Whitehill, in 1707 – the year of the Act of Union with England, for which he was a commissioner. At that stage it was actually called Broughton House, for five years earlier the 2nd Lord Bellenden of Broughton, no Croesus himself, had picked it up from its bankrupt builder, James Smith. The wretched architect's financial plight can be explained by the fact that he and his wife had no less than two-dozen children.

As built by him in about 1686, the seven-bay Whitehill would hardly have been big enough to accommodate Smith's ever-expanding brood. Nonetheless, the design of his pioneering Palladian villa (Howard Colvin, never an authority given to superlatives, has gone so far as to describe Whitehill as the first real instance of an understanding of Palladian architecture in Great Britain) is a fascinating precursor of the celebrated palaces he went on to build: Hamilton (the ducal seat demolished in the 1920s) and Dalkeith (a property of the Dukes of Buccleuch now let out to an American university).

The shell of Smith's late 17th-century Whitehill survives, together with his wonderfully twisting spiral staircase (complete with robust wrought-iron balustrade by William Aitken) and the wainscoting in the Chinese Room, originally the parlour. What we see at Newhailes today, though, is predominantly the result of the Dalrymples' radical remodelling and redecoration of the 18th century.

Like so many great Scots families, the Dalrymples' fortunes were founded in the Law. Sir David Dalrymple, Newhailes' new owner, was a younger son of the 1st Viscount of Stair, President of the Court of Session, and his elder brother, John (later 1st Earl of Stair), made his name as Lord Justice Clerk – before earning notoriety as the Joint Secretary of State who authorized the treacherous massacre of the Clan Macdonald at Glencoe in 1692. This barbarous act led to the Dalrymples' armorial bearings, the Nine of Diamonds, becoming known as 'the Curse of Scotland'.

ABOVE The Dining Room, painted by James
Norie in 1739 in 'olive oyl' and bewitchingly
unchanged.

RIGHT View through doorway of the Entrance
Hall, which contains some of Thomas Clayton's
best plasterwork (of 1742).

Whatever the malignance of Lord Stair, though, there was nothing cursed
about Newhailes. Far from being a haunt of evil, it became the epitome of
the 18th-century Enlightenment, with a famous Library memorably described
by Dr Samuel Johnson as 'the most learned room in Europe'.

The Library wing was begun by Sir David Dalrymple shortly before his death
in 1721. Its designer remains an intriguing mystery. Until recently it had always
been assumed it was William Adam who was responsible for extending Smith's
original block to the east (Library wing) and west (Dining Room wing). Yet
now John Cornforth has come up with the startling suggestion that Sir David
may have consulted James Gibbs, the most experienced Classical architect of the
day, on one of his frequent visits to London.

In any event, Sir David's dream of enlarging Newhailes was realized with
consummate style by his son and successor, Sir James. A pretty new entrance
hall was created which was adorned with delightful plasterwork by Thomas
Clayton, complete with ornate swags, flowers, birds, trophies and – a particularly
nice touch – lions' manes fluttering in the Forth breeze. The Dining Room
extension was ingeniously disguised by a screen of two pairs of Ionic columns.

Behind them glass panels of bevelled Vauxhall plate enhance a brilliant piece of dramatic design.

This room was painted by James Norie in 1739, in a seductive shade of olive green 'oyl'. Under the sway of the constant maritime theme at Newhailes (there are even carvings of knotted rope around the doorcases in the Drawing Room), one found oneself thinking of Olive Oyl and Popeye the Sailorman.

The most eye-popping interiors of all come in the east wing. First, of course, the Library, which was enriched by Sir James with a splendid new marble chimneypiece (unattributed, though the great Sir Henry Cheere provided three others in the house, these being the only Cheere chimneypieces in Scotland) and a plaster overmantel by Clayton framing Sir John Medina's double-portrait of Sir James as a boy with his father. The Library enjoyed its zenith in the time of Sir James's own son, another Sir David, better known by his Session title of Lord Hailes, who wrote *The Annals of Scotland* (Samuel Smith, 1743, £15) on the mahogany writing table here. Lord Hailes was described in *Douglas's Peerage* as 'that honour to his country and to human nature'; and by way of an illustration that Dr Johnson's immortal remark about his library was no rodomontade, the philosopher David Hume once asked the owner of Newhailes for a copy of *The Life of Oliver Cromwell,* which he could not find in the Advocates Library in Edinburgh. Lord Hailes's book collection contained some 7,000 volumes packed from floor to ceiling.

It is a measure of Newhailes's extraordinary spirit that this noble room still has a potent atmosphere even though the towering shelves are now actually empty of books. The collection was accepted by the Treasury in lieu of tax on the late Sir Mark Dalrymple's estate in the 1970s and placed in the National Library of Scotland. The likely return of the volumes to the shelves in due course

is one of the most exciting prospects offered by Newhailes's reincarnation as a National Trust for Scotland showplace.

The showing of the amazing China Closet off the Library – a cornucopia of porcelain of almost every conceivable description packed into a claustrophobic corner – will present particular logistical problems for the Trust. This astonishing arrangement, as well as (presumably) the gold surround in the Library overmantel, the alterations to Norie's panels in the Chinese Room, and much else besides, belong to the hitherto underrated contribution made to Newhailes during the 19th century.

Students of country-house life will wait with interest to see what the NTS can uncover about this period. Lord Hailes's redoubtable spinster daughter, Christian Dalrymple, a staunch philanthropist and friend to the local miners' wives, ruled at Newhailes for nearly 50 years. When a young man had the impertinence to ask the hunchbacked old lady why she had never married, Miss Dalrymple modestly responded, 'Much to the credit of mankind, no one has ever asked me.'

Christian's nephew and successor, Sir Charles Dalrymple Fergusson, 5th Bt of Kilkerran, called in William Burn to make various improvements in 1839, a year after his aunt's death. Further changes were made later in the 19th century by his younger son, Charles, who took the name of Dalrymple and was given a new baronetcy (his elder brother succeeded to Kilkerran and the Fergusson title). Some of these were unfortunate, especially the substitution of plate-glass (and poor plate-glass, at that) for a few of the classical sash windows. Replacing the proper fenestration will help to rejuvenate the frankly dilapidated facade and should rank high in the National Trust for Scotland's heroic crusade to preserve the magic of Newhailes for posterity.

LEFT James Smith's original winding staircase of *circa* 1686.

BELOW The entrance front, framed by Palladian gatepiers. To the original seven-bay villa of the late 1680s was added, to the right, the Library wing of 1719–20 and, to the left, the wing containing the 'Great Apartment' of rooms, completed in 1733. The plate-glass windows on the first floor were an unsympathetic Victorian addition (and it is hoped that they will be replaced).

12

YESTER HOUSE

EAST LOTHIAN

A T MOST great houses the past casts a long shadow, but at Yester on the edge of the Lammermuir Hills, nothwithstanding its long history as a family seat stretching back to at least the 13th century, the future demands to take centre-stage. For the present owner, Gian Carlo Menotti, the eminent operatic composer who bought Yester in 1972, has laid elaborate plans for an international theatre school on the estate – complete with a projected modern theatre in the Classical style designed by the architect Quinlan Terry. A model of the theatre, incorporating the existing and now derelict stable block beyond the walled gardens, catches one's eye in the entrance hall at Yester and the Maestro's exciting vision, formally launched here in 1992 by the Prince of Wales, adds vibrant tone to the Menottis' magnificent family home.

One of Maestro Menotti's many operas was entitled *The Boy Who Grew Too Fast* and an architectural purist might argue that Yester itself is a house that grew too fast, or at least one that was altered too many times for absolute perfection. The present building was originally designed, with delicate Classical restraint, by James Smith, whom we encountered at Newhailes (*qv*), at the end of the 17th century. Too quickly, one might say, it was robustly interfered with by William Adam in the early 18th century and then further altered by his sons – though here the argument rather falls apart for Robert Adam's Saloon of 1789 must, by any standards, rank as one of the greatest interiors in Scotland. Next came 19th-century 'improvements' which culminated in a new entrance, plus *porte-cochère*, to the west and a radical rearrangement of the interior to accommodate a new entrance hall.

Yet, for all the changes, Yester indubitably remains a sensational, and surprisingly little-known, great house. For centuries it was the seat of the Hay family, Marquesses of Tweeddale, who inherited the estate in the 14th century through marriage to the Gifford heiress. The Giffords had been here since Norman times and built the old castle, the ruins of which are about a mile to

the south-east of the present house. The local legend that the castle's 13th-century builder, Hugo Gifford, had been in league with the Devil was immortalized in Sir Walter Scott's *Marmion* (in the Host's Tale). Hugo's sunken 'Goblin Hall', a vaulted chamber 37 feet long, is still in existence.

By the end of the 16th century, the Hays had moved to a new house more or less on the present site. This appears to have been a four-storey tower house, with later gabled wings, facing the Gifford Water. In the 17th century formal gardens were laid out and extensive planting carried out to enhance the glorious natural setting that Yester enjoys to this day.

This ambitious landscaping was presumably the responsibility of John Hay, 2nd Earl and 1st Marquess of Tweeddale, who inherited the estate in 1653. A shrewd statesman, John was a remarkable survivor in the stormy politics of the time; having sat in two Cromwellian Parliaments he went on to serve Kings Charles II, James VII and II and William III, ending up as Lord Chancellor of Scotland. Along the way he emerged relatively unscathed, if financially damaged, from a falling-out with his son's father-in-law, the powerful Duke of Lauderdale, of Thirlestane Castle (*qv*).

Away from political intrigue, the 1st Marquess of Tweeddale was a man of taste and a member of the Royal Society. He consulted the 'Architect Royal', Sir William Bruce, about a plan for a new house at Yester but in the event it

ABOVE The south (garden) front. William Adam's addition of a raised 'temple roof' sits a little uneasily with James Smith's admittedly leaking original.

PRECEDING PAGES 'The finest room at least in Scotland, and few equal to it in England,' predicted the Scottish history painter Gavin Hamilton of the Saloon to the 4th Marquess of Tweeddale in 1755. The finished article, a splendid example of the Adam family's work with its coffered ceiling, hardly falls short of Hamilton's prediction. The wall paintings, though, are not by Hamilton himself but by William Delacour (1761).

was left to his son, the 2nd Marquess, to tackle the project with Bruce's successor as Overseer of the Royal Works, James Smith. In 1697, immediately after the 1st Marquess's death, Smith and his partner Alexander McGill drew up the plans. Although the original drawings have yet to come to light, William Adam's *Vitruvius Scoticus* shows a plan for Yester with a strong resemblance to Bruce's own scheme at Kinross (*qv*).

Although, viewed through the broad sweep of history, Yester may seem to have been chopped and changed too frequently, in reality the original building work was painfully slow. By the time the 4th Marquess of Tweeddale inherited Yester in 1715, while still a minor, work had ground to a halt. From the 1720s onwards, though, Lord Tweeddale set about transforming the restrained Baroque design – a little French in inspiration, as Alistair Rowan has pointed out – into a Rococo house.

In view of Yester's current musical celebrity, it is instructive to read in John Macky's *Journey Through Scotland* (1723) that, 'You enter the body of the house up six or eight steps into a large hall 36 foot high, and behind it a Salon fronting the garden of the same height, and at top is a gallery for Musick, exactly as at Blenheim.'

While the centre block was being built Lord Tweeddale and his mother lived in the flanking pavilions – only one of which, alas, now survives. Unfortunately,

BELOW The new entrance hall to the west, created for the 8th Marquess of Tweeddale by Robert Brown in the 1830s. A model of Quinlan Terry's scheme for the conversion of the derelict stables into Gian Carlo Menotti's brainchild, the Yester Theatre School, can be seen on the table between the two Ionic columns.

ABOVE LEFT View up to the ceiling of the Staircase Hall, showing plasterwork by Joseph Enzer.

ABOVE and ABOVE RIGHT Details of plasterwork by Enzer in the Staircase Hall (*above*) and Dining Room (*above right*).

RIGHT The Dining Room, originally William Adam's entrance hall, which was converted to its present purpose in the 1830s.

by the time Smith's 'body of the house' was finally completed in the 1720s it struck the new Lord Tweeddale as rather old-fashioned. Moreover, the roof leaked.

In 1729 William Adam was called up to remedy the problem. The architect introduced a type of 'temple roof' he had seen at Colen Campbell's Wanstead on a recent tour of England, and pressed Lord Tweeddale to undertake all manner of other alterations. Lord Tweeddale, a lawyer who knew his own mind (he eventually became Lord Justice-General of Scotland), sternly resisted some of Adam's more exuberant exterior proposals but gave him a fairly free hand inside.

Today, the main William Adam interiors that have survived the alterations of Robert Adam in the 1700s and Robert Brown in the 1830s are the Staircase and the old entrance hall (now the Dining Room). Both these superb spaces are wonderfully adorned by the plasterwork of Joseph Enzer, who also worked with William Adam at Arniston (*qv*) and the House of Dun (*qv*). The Staircase, with its coved ceiling, is enlivened by a riot of Rococo cartouches, voluted scrolls, acanthus sprouts and garlands. The plasterwork in the Dining Room is more light-hearted: busts of the four Seasons in the corners, Jupiter and Ganymede above each fireplace.

A lighter mood in general arrived at Yester when the bachelor 4th Marquess, by then in his mid-fifties, married Lady Frances Carteret in 1748. John Adam, the eldest son of William (who died in the same year) was kept busy converting the east wing into nurseries for the six children the new Marchioness bore in five years.

Another marriage, in the mid-1780s, between the 7th Marquess of Tweeddale and Lady Hannah Maitland, brought about further changes at Yester. Encouraged by his wife, accustomed to the palatial grandeur of Thirlestane (*qv*), this Marquess of comparatively humble birth (his maternal grandfather was described in *The Complete Peerage* as 'a labourer' from Lancashire), who inherited the title unexpectedly from a distant kinsman, decided that yet

more improvements were needed at Yester. These involved Robert Adam designing a new neo-Classical scheme to refront the north and south fronts.

In the event, only the north front was executed, after Robert Adam's death in 1792. The pity of this slightly botched operation was that William Adam's elegant external staircase to the entrance hall was replaced by a clumsy ramp. Nonetheless, Robert deserves the credit for replacing the original small windows of his father's design for the Saloon in 1789 by the high arched openings that give this stupendous room its air of lightness.

The origins of Robert Adam's version of the Saloon go back to the early 1760s, when he and his brother John chose William Delacour, first master of the Edinburgh School of Design, to paint the vast, tapestry-like canvases which still decorate the room today. The identity of the stuccodore responsible for the plasterwork remains unknown.

Back in 1755, the Scottish history painter Gavin Hamilton gave the 4th Marquess of Tweeddale the benefit of his advice on the proposed Saloon:

> I am entirely of the Italian way of thinking, viz: that there can be
> no true magnificence without the assistance of either painting or
> sculpture and I will venture to say that if this room is finished in
> the manner that I propose it will be the finest room at least in
> Scotland, and few equal to it in England.

Thanks to Robert Adam, the result is surely not far short of Hamilton's bold claim.

ABOVE View through Saloon from first-floor landing.

RIGHT Maestro Menotti's exuberant studio on the first floor, with, to the left, an 18th-century Italian organ case.

Ten years after Robert Adam's death, the 7th Marquess and his wife somewhat unwisely chose France as a place to recuperate from the rigours of a Scottish winter. They were promptly imprisoned by Napoleon and their supposed health cure soon ended in their deaths at Verdun.

Their colourful son, the 8th Marquess of Tweeddale, dominated Yester's 19th-century history. An aggressively hearty soldier, who eventually rose to the rank of Field Marshal and served a long stint as Governor of Madras, the 8th Marquess entered Lothian folklore as a tireless exponent of tile-draining,

The Drawing Room, formerly the garden parlour on the south front, was refitted by Robert Brown with a new fireplace and coffered ceiling 'quite in the present style' (the 1830s). Today the Menottis have decorated the room in a charmingly Italianate manner.

deep ploughing and other agricultural experiments. Stories abound of his pugilistic prowess – one has him wrestling with the Gifford blacksmith, who declined to give way to His Lordship on a bridge, before throwing this stalwart of the forge into a ditch – and his skill with the whip. Known as 'the Prince of the Heavy Bays', he once drove the mail-coach from London to Haddington 'at a sitting'. The horses' opinion of the 8th Marquess would doubtless have been not dissimilar to that of his mature son and heir, who was bawled out by the old boy for daring to use his father's personal door to the Dining Room.

The conversion of the old entrance hall to the Dining Room and the creation of a new entrance hall to the west were merely two of the 8th Marquess's myriad alterations at Yester. Less happy was the demolition of the west wing, thereby disturbing the house's symmetry. The old garden parlour on the south front was refitted by Robert Brown as a Drawing Room in 1830, with a coffered ceiling 'quite in the present style'. Something of the 8th Marquess's relationship with the unfortunate Brown can be deduced from the latter's plea to his patron 'to have the goodness to address me, architect'.

After the end of the Hay family's long tenure some 30 years ago, Yester was briefly the residence of Mr Peter Morris and Mr Derek Parker, two antiques experts. The credit for the present superb state of the house must go to Gian Carlo Menotti's son, Francis, who not only redecorated and refurnished every room but also – with the help of Historic Scotland – installed a new roof and gave the Saloon a new floor. In addition, he conceived and executed the charming Print Room. The Maestro's airy studio on the first floor contains a gorgeous Italian organ case and the Drawing Room underneath has a romantically Italianate feel. The Saloon makes a marvellous setting for music – and the stable block cries out for the fulfilment of the Maestro's dream, which would make Yester as internationally celebrated in the world of music as Spoleto, the festival Gian Carlo Menotti founded nearly 40 years ago.

View to the south from the terrace on the entrance front. William Adam's elegant external staircase which formerly led up to this balustrade was replaced in the late 18th century by a less happy ramp.

13

HOPETOUN
HOUSE

IF PUT on the spot and asked to single out a 'Great House' in Scotland, one would have to choose Hopetoun, the largest and most sensational country house of its kind north of the border. With its vast forecourt and sweeping, curved colonnades, this Baroque palace of the Hope family, Earls of Hopetoun and latterly Marquesses of Linlithgow, has understandably been called 'the Scottish Versailles'.

Not the least of Hopetoun's thrills is its proximity to the Firth of Forth, and the sea. The late Lady Victoria Wemyss, who died aged 104 in 1994, recalled dining at Hopetoun one evening in 1916 when she heard the eerie rattle of chains outside in the Firth. The party went up to the roof terrace and watched the Fleet weighing anchor before setting out for the Battle of Jutland. Lady Victoria (Queen Victoria's last surviving godchild and a second cousin of Queen Elizabeth The Queen Mother) remembered some of the ladies waving their underskirts to wish the men God speed. She remembered, too, that when the Fleet returned there were empty spaces in their formations at anchor.

As a boy in the 1950s our photographer remembers the excitement of staying at Hopetoun and being able to see the Forth Railway Bridge from his bedroom on the nursery floor. Today the amazing view from the roof terrace also takes in the new Forth Road Bridge – a striking example of how modern structures can actually enhance, rather than spoil, stately prospects.

The sea could be said to have played a crucial part in the history of Hopetoun. The family tradition goes that in 1682 John Hope of Hopetoun – who four years earlier had bought the estate on which the present house stands from the Setons – lost his life in a shipwreck through giving up his seat in a lifeboat to the Duke of York (later King James VII of Scotland and II of England). According to one account of the sinking of the frigate *Gloucester*, the Duke's dogs were also saved but poor Hope and several other gallant Scots gentlemen who were in attendance perished.

By way of compensation, as it were, Queen Anne created John Hope of Hopetoun's son and successor, Charles, Earl of Hopetoun when he came of age in 1703. The fortunes of the Hope family – a respectable dynasty of Edinburgh merchants, lawyers and courtiers – had been handsomely consolidated by John's father, Sir James Hope, an expert mineralogist who skilfully exploited the lead mines inherited by his wife, Anne Foulis, in Lanarkshire.

After John Hope had drowned, the development of his new estate at Hopetoun was left in the capable hands of his widow, Lady Margaret, eldest daughter of the 4th Earl of Haddington. The architect chosen was Sir William Bruce, the Palladian pioneer and hero of the chapter on Kinross House (*qv*). From 1699 onwards he built a deliciously restrained, urbane gentleman's seat in the Classical manner. This would surely have earned him an even greater claim to posterity had not Lady Margaret's son Charles – under the influence of his flamboyant brother-in-law, the 2nd Marquess of Annandale – decided to make a bigger splash with the help of William Adam.

Today Hopetoun tends to be thought of as an Adam house – naturally enough, as it is not only one of William's chief works but also a significant staging-post for his son, the great Robert, whose courtyard pavilions and their remarkable towers are among his earliest independent commissions. From the front, it is Adam all the way – and very magnificent it is too. Yet, walk round to the back and you will see that Bruce's quiet voice, reticent and dignified, can still be heard, emanating from the perfectly proportioned west, or garden, front. In the eyes of many discerning architectural judges this side of Hopetoun is the more satisfactory of the two.

Inside the house, as well, the Adams did not carry everything before them. The panelled Garden Parlour, the Libraries and the Bruce Bedchamber (designed for the young 1st Earl of Hopetoun) all still evoke Sir William's exquisite late 17th-century taste, as does the main staircase, with its luscious carving by Alexander Eizart, who worked with Bruce, the 'Architect Royal', at the Palace of Holyroodhouse.

PRECEDING PAGES Detail of William Adam's east front, showing steps and colonnade.

ABOVE Rooftop view of the north pavilion, with the Firth of Forth in the background.

RIGHT Sir William Bruce's pine-panelled staircase with elaborate carvings by Alexander Eizart, who worked with the Architect Royal at Holyroodhouse. The hand-rail and banisters are of oak. The neo-Classical murals are modern, being painted in 1967 by the Scottish *trompe l'oeil* artist William McLaren as a memorial to the first Marchioness of the 3rd Marquess, the former Vivien Kenyon-Slaney from Hatton Grange, Shropshire, who died in 1963. They reflect Lady Linlithgow's love of Hopetoun and its variety of wildlife.

BELOW Sir William Bruce's west (garden) front.

ABOVE Enfilade through State rooms.

RIGHT The Yellow Drawing Room, originally the State Dining Room, with joinery by the Hopetoun estate craftsman John Paterson, stucco ceiling by John Dawson and furniture by James Cullen. The large painting on the left is *The Adoration of the Shepherds* (School of Rubens). The Scottish artist Henry Raeburn was knighted in this room by King George IV during his visit to Hopetoun in 1822.

The seeds of the brevity of Bruce's house at Hopetoun were sown in the same year as he began building operations, for in 1699 the 17-year-old Charles Hope of Hopetoun married Lady Henrietta Johnston, only daughter of the 1st Marquess of Annandale. Lady Henrietta's precocious connoisseur brother, James, later the 2nd Marquess of Annandale, had strong views on architecture and urged his brother-in-law to think big. He himself had remodelled another Bruce house, at Craighall, Fife, to the designs of William Adam, an adventurous Classical architect inspired by the dramatic styles of Sir John Vanbrugh and James Gibbs. Adam – who is said to have been apprenticed to Bruce at Hopetoun as a boy in the early 1700s – made his name with the publication of his first volume of *Vitruvius Scoticus* in 1720.

The next year – in which Charles Hopetoun's bachelor brother-in-law also happened to succeed to the Marquessate of Annandale – William Adam began transforming Bruce's house at Hopetoun. Bruce had built a grand entrance forecourt but within a mere 20 years this was to be swept away for something even grander. First of all, Adam extended one wing; then, in 1725, he began the colonnades; and in 1727 came the plan for a completely new facade.

The fabulous scale of Adam's new entrance front is emphasized by the extravagant use of the fluted giant pilasters. The original design had proposed a central portico and a curved double stairway but these were never built, presumably on grounds of economy. The broad stone steps that were built are all the more impressive on account of their noble simplicity.

The stonework of the great new house was not completed until 1748, the year of William Adam's death. Lord Annandale did not live to see its completion, as he died of consumption aged 42 in Naples, but he bequeathed his outstanding art collection to his brother-in-law, the 1st Earl of Hopetoun, who survived another 12 years. Lord Annandale is commemorated at Hopetoun in an appropriately flamboyant Baroque portrait by Andrea Procaccini which

ABOVE Sunlight and shade in the Small Library in the Bruce part of the house.

LEFT The Red Drawing Room, with Rococo ceiling executed for John Adam by John Dawson, a Scots plasterer whom the architect had encountered in London. The marble chimneypiece was ordered by Robert Adam, then in Rome, and carved in 1756 by Michael Rysbrack. The furniture was supplied by James Cullen *circa* 1766.

RIGHT The Bruce Bedchamber, originally part of a suite designed by Sir William Bruce for the young Charles Hope, later 1st Earl of Hopetoun. The gilded wall paintings (of 1791–2) are by James Norie, the Edinburgh decorator, who also worked at Newhailes (*qv*). The State bed was supplied in 1768 by Mathias Lock of London for the Great Bedchamber (now subsumed in the State Dining Room).

hangs in the State Dining Room near a significantly less flamboyant study of the 1st Earl of Hopetoun by David Allan, with the house in the background.

When the 2nd Earl of Hopetoun inherited the property in 1742, William Adam's newly recast 'Great Apartment', the enfilade of State rooms running north from the entrance hall, was still an unfinished shell. The decoration and furnishing of these rooms was to extend over 26 years and to deploy the talents of William Adam's sons, Robert and John. They were responsible for the pretty Rococo coved ceilings in the Green Dining Room (now the Yellow Drawing Room) and the Red Drawing Room with plasterwork by John Dawson.

The 2nd Earl was so pleased with Robert Adam's work that in 1754 he suggested the young architect should accompany his brother Charles on an Italian tour and share expenses. This celebrated trip – despite its lack of harmony, with Adam complaining that he had to bear most of the expenses while Hope took all the credit – was to have far-reaching effects on the course of architecture in Britain. Its immediate consequence at Hopetoun was the great marble chimneypiece in the Red Drawing Room, the design of which was sent by Robert Adam from Rome. It was carved by Michael Rysbrack.

Adam also designed the Rococo console tables in the same room. Most of the mid-Georgian furniture at Hopetoun was supplied by James Cullen of the Edinburgh Upholstery Company. Unfortunately, the pier tables in the Red Drawing Room were made to the wrong dimensions and portions of the architrave had to be cut out to accommodate them. The seat furniture in this room was made by Thomas Welsh, a carver recommended ('may also turn out usefull') by Sir James Dalrymple of Newhailes (*qv*).

The final room in the Great Apartment, the State Dining Room, was created early in the 19th century by combining the old Ante-Chamber and Great Bedchamber. This was done for General the 4th Earl of Hopetoun, a Peninsular War commander, to the designs of the architect James Gillespie Graham. The General, who also added greatly to Hopetoun's collection of Old Master paintings, entertained King George IV on his famous visit to Edinburgh in 1822. The King, no mean builder himself, was suitably impressed by Hopetoun – 'By *Gad*, you've got big pleasures,' he observed of Adam's landscaped 'policies' – even if he lunched only modestly off turtle soup and three glasses of wine.

Subsequent Earls of Hopetoun continued to improve their estates and then, in the late 19th and early 20th centuries, the family became prominent in international affairs when the 7th Earl, later the 1st Marquess of Linlithgow, served as the first Governor-General of the Commonwealth of Australia and the 2nd Marquess of Linlithgow as Viceroy and Governor-General of India. Full-length portraits of these pro-consular figures dominate the coolly Palladian Entrance Hall at Hopetoun and their Imperial experiences add lustre to the mementoes in the Family Museum.

The 3rd Marquess of Linlithgow was taken prisoner at Dunkirk in 1940 with the 51st Highland Division and ended up in the Nazi fortress of Colditz as one of the 'Prominente'. In 1974 he and his son, the Earl of Hopetoun (now the 4th Marquess), were instrumental in setting up an independent charitable trust to preserve Hopetoun House with its historic contents and surrounding landscape for the benefit of the public. The Preservation Trust has done much good work in educating the young to appreciate Hopetoun's heritage.

The State Dining Room, created in the early 19th century by, in all probability, James Gillespie Graham, who combined the old Ante-Chamber and Great Bedchamber. The original doors and architraves of the earlier rooms were reused as part of a lavish Regency ensemble, complete with gilt wallpaper and a gilded cornice and sunburst ceiling rose.

ABOVE View of the Forth road and rail bridges from Hopetoun's roof.

LEFT The Entrance Hall, remodelled in the early 1750s by John Adam, William's eldest son. The full-length portrait above the chimneypiece is of the 7th Earl of Hopetoun, who became the 1st Marquess of Linlithgow, in Thistle robes. He was the first Governor-General of the Commonwealth of Australia.

Fortunately the house and its spacious outbuildings – such as the vast Ballroom in the south pavilion, which was originally a library and then a riding school – are ideally suited to the large-scale corporate entertaining so vital to the modern economy of great houses.

The passion for present-day life in a great house which Hopetoun generates among all those involved in its management is reflected in the active conservation work being undertaken by the Hopetoun House Preservation Trust. The National Heritage Memorial Fund has recently funded the acquisition of most of the contents of this great treasure-house by the Trust, which is ensuring that were the 2nd Earl of Hopetoun to return today he would find his family seat by the Forth in good hands.

14

MELLERSTAIN

BERWICKSHIRE

A T THIS stage of the narrative we have emphatically arrived in the Age of Adam. Mellerstain – an enchanting 18th-century 'toy fort' in the Borders which, understandably, many architectural enthusiasts regard affectionately as their favourite great house in Scotland – is an especially instructive example for it allows us to contrast the architectural styles of Father and Son, William and Robert.

Mellerstain was built in two distinct stages: first came the wings in 1725 from William Adam and then, some half-a-century later, the large central block by Robert. As one enters the spacious forecourt the difference is apparent enough, with the projection in the centre being a typically bold flourish of the younger Adam. By contrast, the south facade at the back, looking out over the Edwardian formal gardens to the cheviots, is flatter and more subtle.

For all its jolly castellated skyline and the warmth of its local yellowish stone, Mellerstain strikes some visitors as a little severe. Inside, though, Robert Adam really let rip. The results can hardly fail to inspire the most curmudgeonly critic. The ceilings, friezes and fireplaces sing with a refreshingly cool, classical assurance.

There can be no lovelier interior in Scotland than the Library at Mellerstain with its Adam bookcases (which undoubtedly 'furnish the room') and green-and-white marble chimneypiece. The gaily coloured ceiling of 1770, adorned with Minerva and representations of 'Teaching' and 'Learning' by Zucci, is rightly considered one of Robert Adam's masterpieces. Another splendid ceiling, dated three years later and decorated with eagles and sphinxes, is to be found at the centre of the garden enfilade in the Music Room, which Robert Adam originally designed as a dining room.

The family portraits in this room of Baillies, Humes and Hamiltons help bring Mellerstain's genealogy to life. The Baillie family acquired the estate in 1642 when George Baillie, son of a prosperous Edinburgh merchant, was granted

PRECEDING PAGES The entrance front: the central block is by Robert Adam, the wings by his father, William.

RIGHT The Library: one of Robert Adam's outstanding creations, with an exquisite decorated ceiling in the original colours of 1773. The circular oil painting of Minerva is by Zucci. The high-backed chair in the foreground is William and Mary period, *circa* 1700.

BELOW Enfilade through State rooms.

a Royal Charter. Originally a property of the Haliburtons, Mellerstain later belonged to the Haitlie family, one of whom was killed in a feud in 1603. The house here, known as Whiteside (and described as 'ane auld melancholic hous that had had great buildings about it'), seems to have stood not far from the present site – indeed it may well have survived for a while as a ruin between William Adam's two new wings, which may account for the curious time-lapse of nearly 50 years before the main block was built.

During the religious troubles of the 17th century the Baillies were staunch Covenanters and in 1676 Robert Baillie, George's son and successor, was imprisoned and fined the then huge sum of £500 for rescuing his brother-in-law (also a Johnston cousin) from what he thought to be illegal arrest. As Robert languished in the Tolbooth in Edinburgh, he was visited in jail by the plucky Grisell Hume, 12-year-old daughter of his political ally and local MP, Sir Patrick Hume, 2nd Bt. Sir Patrick had entrusted a secret message to this determined young go-between who was to play a leading role in the saga of Mellerstain. The romantic story goes that young Grisell met her future husband, George Baillie, Robert's

ABOVE and ABOVE RIGHT Robert Adam's beautifully proportioned Front Hall, with its apsidal ends.

RIGHT The armorial bearings of the Baillie-Hamiltons, Earls of Haddington.

son, while he happened to be visiting his father in the Tolbooth at the same time as her own brave mission.

Many vicissitudes had to be endured before they could marry and settle at Mellerstain. In 1684 Robert Baillie was executed for high treason and the Mellerstain estate was forfeited. The Hume estate of Polwarth (where Sir Patrick had once avoided arrest by hiding for a month in the family vault) suffered a similar fate the next year when Sir Patrick himself was extremely fortunate not to end with his head on the block for his part in the Monmouth Rebellion. Even such a staid authority as *The Complete Peerage* felt moved to observe that 'this turbulent scoundrel' should have done so. Thomas Macaulay muttered that Hume's name had often been mentioned in his *History* 'and never mentioned with honour'.

In any event, the Humes took off for Holland where they were joined by Grisell's young friend George Baillie. Times were hard, and owing to the poor health of her mother, the burden of managing the impoverished refugee household fell upon Grisell, the eldest girl of no less than 18 children. Her

LEFT The main staircase, which rises in two flights and proceeds in one.

RIGHT The corner of the Drawing Room, showing Allan Ramsay's portrait of Rachel Hamilton and her brother Charles, 1740. They were children of Lord Binning and his wife, Rachel Baillie, the ultimate heiress of Mellerstain.

remarkable housekeeping skills were to form the basis for her *Household Book,* which was eventually published and hailed as a classic of Scottish social history. What her father Sir Patrick Hume wrote of her mother, a Miss Carre of Cavers, could equally well have applied to their indomitable daughter: 'a grave majestic countenance, a composed steady and mild spirit, of a most firm and equal mind, never elevated by prosperity, nor debased nor daunted by adversity'.

Sir Patrick's remarks about his wife's 'plump full body' and 'clear ruddy complexion' would not, however, have been appropriate for Grisell. The portrait of her by Maria Verelst which hangs in the Front Hall at Mellerstain shows a most elegant figure, though not without a steely streak.

In Holland Grisell knew despair – 'And were na my heart licht I wad dee', she wrote in a ballad – but also love. She and George were finally married in 1691 by which time the Hume and Baillie estates had been restored – and her father, by now Lord Polwarth (and eventually Earl of Marchmont), was riding high in the favour of King William III.

George Baillie of Mellerstain went on to become an MP and one of the architects of the Act of Union with England in 1707. For the architecture of a new house in keeping with his status he and Lady Grisell (as she became styled when her father was elevated to the Earldom of Marchmont in 1697) turned to William Adam, fresh down from his triumphs at Hopetoun (*qv*) and already established as Scotland's leading Classical architect. Adam drew up plans for a Palladian centre-piece (curiously, never built) with two wings. The foundation stone of the east wing, was laid on September 11, 1725.

The original scheme provided for the two wings to be connected by corridors, but as built there was nothing between them – except perhaps the ruins of old Whiteside. The two wings were, though, fine houses in themselves and survive as interesting examples of Scottish architecture of an earlier epoch, with their wide-spaced windows, solid stone dressings and broad, satisfying surfaces of rough cast.

It is pleasant to imagine Lady Grisell and her family living contentedly here in the 1720s after all the traumas of the past. By all accounts she and George were a devoted couple. 'They never had the shadow of a quarrel or misunderstanding or dryness betwixt them, not for a moment,' recalled their elder daughter, Lady Murray. 'He never went abroad but she went to the window to look after him, and so she did that very day he fell ill the last time he went abroad, never taking her eyes from him as long as he was in sight.'

George Baillie died in 1738, to be followed eight years later by Lady Grisell. Mellerstain eventually passed to their grandson, George Hamilton, second son of their younger daughter, Rachel, who married Lord Binning, heir of the 6th Earl of Haddington. The Hamiltons, Earls of Haddington, had been one of the most prosperous dynasties in Scotland since the early 17th century when Sir Thomas Hamilton, an eminent lawyer who became 1st Lord Binning and 1st Earl of Haddington, developed the mines on his estates and acquired extensive Abbey lands, such as Tyninghame.

As it turned out, Rachel's husband Lord Binning – author of a pastoral poem intriguingly entitled 'Ungrateful Nanny' – never succeeded to the Earldom of Haddington, dying of consumption in Naples aged 35. Their elder son, Thomas, inherited the Earldom and the paternal estates; the younger son, George, came into the maternal property of Mellerstain and took the name Baillie.

The new George Baillie of Mellerstain was a man of taste, having done the Grand Tour, and naturally turned to William Adam's fashionable son, Robert, to complete the house his grandparents had started in 1725. It is clear from the plans, copiously initialled 'G.B.', that Baillie did not give Robert Adam a completely free hand. Here was a client who knew his own mind: he did not want a vast, pretentious palace but a comfortable and elegant country house on a human scale, with just a hint of the castle on the exterior to reflect the swing away from the purely Classical.

ABOVE Detail of door bell.

RIGHT Detail of overdoor on entrance front.

LEFT AND BELOW Details of garden statuary.

Consequently, the creative discipline imposed on Adam produced not one of his over-the-top extravaganzas but an exquisite gem in miniature. The intimacy of the atmosphere at Mellerstain could be said to be a happy tribute to the creative conflict between George Baillie and Robert Adam.

Much as one sympathizes with Baillie, though, and admires his control over Adam, it can only be a matter for regret that the lustrous design for the ceiling of the Great Gallery was never carried out. The barrel vault of this magnificent long room – a wonderful surprise at the top of the house – cries out for Robert Adam's finishing touches. Nonetheless, there is still plenty of delicious detail to enjoy at Mellerstain which has remained joyfully unchanged since Adam completed work here in about 1778.

In 1858 George Baillie's grandson and namesake succeeded his second cousin, the 9th Earl of Haddington, a former Lord Lieutenant of Ireland (who then, rather surprisingly, turned down the Governor-Generalship of India), in the Earldom and assumed the surname of Baillie-Hamilton. Mellerstain's next owner, the 11th Earl of Haddington, a prominent freemason and agriculturalist, brought in the Edwardian architect Sir Reginald Blomfield in 1909 to transform the vista from the garden front. Blomfield, a somewhat pompous Old Haileyburian, has been unfairly derided as a snob keener on the quality of shooting to be had on his client's estates than on the finer points of architecture, but he knew his stuff and at Mellerstain he performed superbly well.

The slope which fell from the south front of the house to the lake at the foot of the hill was ingeniously adapted into a series of garden terraces. Blomfield altered and enlarged the lake – which had been devised in the form of a Dutch canal when George Baillie returned from exile in Holland in the late 17th century – so as to link it to the terraces with a glorious sweep of lawn. The result is a noble composition – seemingly reaching, as the present Earl of Haddington nicely observes, 'to infinity'.

Lord Haddington, a professional photographer celebrated for his pioneering work recording the mysterious rashes of crop circles, has a keen eye for beauty and he and his wife, Jane, have done much to enhance the friendly spirit of Mellerstain. They and their young family live in the west wing, which was converted from its former use as a stable block by the architect Schomberg Scott in 1975. Their informal portraits by Andrew Festing are hung in the Small Drawing Room (originally planned by Robert Adam as a bedchamber) beside those of the late Earl, attired as a gentleman-rider in his racing silks, and his Canadian Countess by Sir Oswald Birley.

Following the death of the late Earl (who was president of the Scottish Georgian Society) in 1986, the new Lord Haddington established a charitable trust to secure the future of Mellerstain. It is a precious, and singularly lovable, jewel for posterity.

ABOVE Mercury by moonlight.

RIGHT East (entrance) front from the terraces, also by moonlight.

15

ARNISTON HOUSE

MIDLOTHIAN

A RNISTON, set in a fine park beneath the Moorfoot Hills and yet only 11 miles south of Edinburgh, deserves to be much better known. With the spirited efforts of its present châtelaine, Althea Dundas Bekker (who shows visitors around), to restore the house after savage outbreaks of dry rot, and the fact that it is now open to the public in the summer months, it surely will be. For it is a splendid example of William Adam's work: a handsome Palladian structure flanked by two wings and containing a breathtaking Baroque hall which automatically puts Arniston in the 'great' class of Scottish country houses.

Adam arrived at Arniston in 1725 after making his mark as a mason at another Midlothian seat, Mavisbank (now a ruin), under the patronage of Sir John Clerk of Penicuik, a noted champion of Palladianism. Clerk took his protégé to see Sir John Vanbrugh's theatrical flourishes at Castle Howard and elsewhere, which greatly excited Adam.

Whereas Sir John Clerk of Penicuik knew precisely what he wanted and kept Adam's new enthusiasms under rigorous control, his next clients, the Dundases of Arniston, a Presbyterian legal dynasty, did not aspire to be arbiters of taste and gave their architect a much freer hand. Nonetheless, Adam was constrained by the Dundas family's desire for the new seat at Arniston to incorporate at least part of the existing, early 17th-century tower-house on the site.

The Dundases had acquired the estate in 1571 at the insistence of the second wife of George Dundas, 16th Laird of Dundas (the ancient seat of the family near Queensferry, West Lothian), Katherine Oliphant, who planned for her son James, to be comfortably set up with a property of his own. The formidable Miss Oliphant is not forgotten at Arniston – though she was remembered less fondly by subsequent Lairds of Dundas itself for her depredations of the main estate to found another one – and a beautiful piece of her embroidery, an elaborate table cover with two Biblical medallions, hangs outside the Oak Room. It is thought to have been completed in about 1595 and features her family's heraldic elephant. (The heralds, like the present writer, can never resist a feeble pun.)

Thanks to his ambitious mama, James Dundas duly established himself at Arniston, built an open courtyard house (though it is possible that the original building pre-dated the purchase of the estate), carried out agricultural improvements and founded a dynasty that achieved almost as much distinction in the Law as the Adam family was to achieve in architecture. Indeed no less than five successive Lairds of Arniston rose to the bench of the Supreme Court of Scotland – an unparalleled record. The creation of the Dundas of the day as a Lord of Session, as 'Lord Arniston', became such a regular event that the peerage might just as well have become hereditary.

The first Lord Arniston, however, James's son and namesake, had to vacate his seat on the bench because he refused to renounce the Covenant. His son Robert – who was ultimately to become the second Lord Arniston – went to live in Holland, where, like so many exiled Scottish landowners, he became enthused by grand ideas concerning European Renaissance architecture. On his return to Arniston after the 'Glorious Revolution' of 1688, when he entered public life as an MP for Midlothian, he began making improvements, particularly in the gardens. Eventually, in 1725, he engaged William Adam to build a new house.

By the time of the old judge's death the next year, though, the building work had progressed no further than the demolition of the enclosing walls of the gardens. It was left to his second son, another Robert and another Lord Arniston,

PRECEDING PAGES The south (garden) front. The coat of arms in the pediment was rescued in the early 1800s from the old Parliament House in Edinburgh by Robert Dundas, the fifth successive head of his family to rise to the bench of the Supreme Court of Scotland.

LEFT and RIGHT Two views of Arniston's magnificent Hall by William Adam with plasterwork by Joseph Enzer, which triumphantly blends the Baroque, Classical and Rococo styles.

to proceed with the Adam project. The elder son, James, had predeceased his father, having landed himself in a spot of bother over a Jacobite medal offered to the Faculty of Advocates by the Duchess of Gordon. James was brought to trial for sedition on account of his apparent enthusiasm for accepting the medal and, although the proceedings were abandoned, the local tradition has it that his irate father, disgusted at his disloyalty to the Crown, had him locked up in a strongroom at Arniston.

Robert, though, was the apple of the old judge's eye and rose with extraordinary rapidity to become first Solicitor-General and then Lord Advocate in his father's lifetime. On inheriting Arniston in 1726, he pressed on with Adam's building work.

Adam partly based his plans on what was already *in situ*. Thus the old house also had a range of buildings which grouped round the main block much as the present pavilions do now. The main hall of the present house incorporates part of the older house, whereas the Oak Room at the back remains as a highly evocative reminder of the 17th-century at Arniston. This atmospheric panelled chamber was one of Sir Walter Scott's favourite interiors. 'I have always loved the old Oak Room at Arniston,' reminisced the author of *The Heart of Midlothian*, 'where I have drunk many a bottle and where I have seen many a hare killed.'

The first part of the new house to be tackled was the Hall, with its spectacular plasterwork by Joseph Enzer, a brilliant Dutch stuccoist whom William Adam was to employ on a number of houses including Yester (*qv*) and the House of Dun (*qv*). Given a free hand to enclose the old baronial 'keep', Adam created an astonishing galleried interior which somehow succeeds in blending the Baroque, Classical and Rococo styles into a harmonious whole. So intensely dramatic is the composition that one experiences difficulty in taking it all in at once; every angle affords a striking new perspective – as our photographer illustrates.

Enzer worked at Arniston for seven years and his exuberant artistry is the house's most memorable delight. Upstairs he was also responsible for the plasterwork in the library, which in the 19th century was converted into a display room, the Porcelain Room, and the books moved downstairs.

Initially the building work went along at a steady rate. Unfortunately, though, the cost of William Adam's elaborate formal gardens – which culminated in a glorious white-stone cascade on the hill behind the house – rather ran away with the budget and in the early 1730s matters came to an abrupt halt, with the west third of the main block incomplete.

The third Lord Arniston, his first family soon to be devastated by smallpox, was in no mood to carry on. The strains of bringing up a new family of nine with his second wife put paid to the prospect of any more expensive architectural indulgences. After a temporary blip in the 1720s, due to his opposition to the Government's Malt Tax (the extremely unpopular 'beer levy'), Robert's legal career took off again and in 1748 he attained the highest office in the judiciary by becoming Lord President of the Court of Session.

His son and namesake, the fourth Lord Arniston, who survived the smallpox epidemic through his absence abroad at Utrecht University, was also to achieve the same prize. Upon inheriting Arniston in 1753, this Robert discovered that the estate was in a great deal of debt. Happily, his first wife, Henrietta Carmichael, was an heiress and her fortune was used to finish off the house.

Every angle of the Hall affords a striking new perspective.

ABOVE Detail of chimneypiece in the John Adam Drawing Room.

LEFT and RIGHT The staircase: porcelain and portraits on the walls.

The architect chosen for the task was William Adam's son John. He altered his father's plans for the internal layout of the uncompleted part of the house by arranging for rooms to be constructed on only two floors instead of three, while keeping within the original facade. This resulted in a splendid drawing room and dining room.

Alas, as Althea Dundas Bekker pointed out, the state of affairs in the early 1990s was that 'Arniston had gone back almost to the 1730s situation'. An outbreak of dry rot in the 1950s had led to the John Adam rooms being stripped of the internal plasterwork and all affected timber, leaving only the external shell. The Drawing Room remains, for the moment at least, a romantic ruin but it is good to report that the Dining Room, with its coved ceiling, has recently been triumphantly restored with the help of grants from Historic Scotland, the national conservation agency.

Among the fourth Lord Arniston's other legacies to the house is the set of terracotta portrait busts which adorn the Porcelain Room. He acquired the busts

The panelled private sitting room on the first floor.

during his vacations at Utrecht University, when he used to tour Italy. Thinking they were just the thing for Arniston, he sent them by sea to Leith.

Indeed portraits are one of Arniston's strongest suits. The exceptionally good collection dates back to the 16th century and includes some robust examples of the work of those two Scots masters Allan Ramsay and Sir Henry Raeburn. They are hung to particular advantage on the staircase where the most celebrated member of the Dundas family, the 1st Viscount Melville, William Pitt's colourful and controversial war minister (described in *The Farington Diary* as 'very hearty, in great spirits, and drinks wine liberally; speaks such broad Scotch that he can hardly be understood') dominates the scene.

Lord Melville was one of the third Lord Arniston's secondary brood of nine children and so a half-brother of the fourth Lord Arniston. The fourth Lord's own son, another Robert (who became Lord Chief Baron of the Exchequer), was the fifth successive head of the family to rise to the bench of the Supreme Court, but declined the Lord Presidency on the grounds of poor health. He did much to improve the Arniston estate, which he adorned with stonework rescued from the demolished Old Parliament House in the early 1800s, and was also responsible for inserting the Scottish coat-of-arms in the pediment on the south side of Arniston House.

The porch on the north side was added in the 1860s by the Chief Baron's grandson, Sir Robert Dundas, 1st Bt, who also heightened the colonnades linking the pavilions to the main part of the house. Inside, he introduced many practical modern conveniences, as well as creating the new ground-floor Library and replacing the stone floor of the Hall with parquet.

In more recent times Arniston has been dogged by bad luck. The roof of the main block had to be completely renewed in the 1980s, the steps leading to the south porch had to be restored and further outbreaks of the dreaded dry rot in various parts of the house have had to be tackled. 'Much work still remains to be done,' admits Althea Dundas Bekker (the eldest daughter of Sir Philip Dundas, 4th Bt), who has been courageously battling away here since the 1970s.

Yet, as the exciting project to restore John Adam's State rooms proceeds, Arniston has the feel of a deeply loved house and we can only be confident of its prospects. Far from being the dour pile of a sober Scots legal dynasty, as one might perhaps expect, it is abundantly full of fun and charm – from Victorian toys in the Old Nursery to the curious old clock in the Hall with its two little old men, reminiscent of medieval garden gnomes, bashing out the chimes with their hammers.

The romantic ruin of the John Adam Drawing Room, ravaged by dry rot in the 1950s.

16

THE HOUSE OF DUN

A S IN THE previous chapter on Arniston (*qv*), the House of Dun, near Montrose, was designed by William Adam for a leading lawyer and adorned with exuberant plasterwork by Joseph Enzer. There, though, the similarity ends for this former seat of the Erskines (now the property of the National Trust for Scotland) does not fit so easily into the pigeon-hole of Classical country houses. The House of Dun is essentially an early 'villa', in the Roman as opposed to the suburban sense of that word, and an exceptionally rare piece of architecture. On these terms alone it demands inclusion among the great houses of Scotland, with the tenure of a colourful, eccentric family and the recent remarkably sympathetic restoration by the National Trust adding lustre to its claims.

The Erskines acquired the estate, overlooking the Montrose Basin, in 1375. Four of the family fell at Flodden, and later in the 16th century the 5th Laird, John Erskine, an associate of John Knox, became Moderator of the General Assembly of the Church of Scotland. He was described as 'a mild sweet-tempered man' by Mary Queen of Scots who found him preferable to most reformers. This may have accounted for his surviving the trip to Paris to attend Mary's wedding to the Dauphin of France; several of the other official commissioners in attendance are supposed to have been poisoned.

Poison certainly played a part in a vicious feud at Dun in the 17th century. Upon the succession of the young 10th Laird, John, in 1610, his wicked Uncle Robert and three demon Aunts plotted to bump off both him and his younger brother, Alexander. The boys were administered the poisoned draught and, as a contemporary account recorded, an extraordinary bout of vomiting ensued, which was so severe that no one expected them to live. John's skin 'turned black and his inward parts were consumed. He continued in great pain and doller to the time of his death.' Uncle Robert and two of his sisters went to the block, while Aunt Helen ('mair penitent though less giltie') was banished to Orkney.

– 167 –

Alexander Erskine, who became 11th Laird, survived this ghastly experience only to die deep in debt in London, his fortune depleted, like those of so many loyal Lairds, by his support for the Royalist cause in the Civil War. The debts were cleared by the next Laird, a canny manager of the estate but there was another family dispute which led to the disinheritance of his two elder sons. In the event, it was the third son, David Erskine, a successful young lawyer, who succeeded to the property in about 1710.

At that time the old tower-house – about a quarter of a mile west of the present house – was still standing. All that remains of this home of the family in the 16th and 17th centuries is an archway in the old walled garden. As Alexander McGill noted, the old castle was 'Raze'd Dow'n to the Ground' by 1723. McGill, the official Edinburgh City Architect, was commissioned by David Erskine – now styled 'Lord Dun' as a Lord of Session – to survey the estate and draw up plans for a new house.

These plans were then passed on to Lord Dun's architectural adviser, the 23rd Earl of Mar, better known as 'Bobbing John', the exiled Jacobite leader then living in France. Lord Dun looked up to him as the head of the Erskine family and, together with his friend Lord Grange (Bobbing John's brother), went so far as to buy the attainted Earl's estate, clear it of debt and then entail it on the Mar heirs. Bobbing John, who fancied himself as an amateur architect and had (according to the Master of Sinclair) a 'malicious, meddling spirit', delighted in pouring scorn over McGill's efforts. He considered McGill's design of the house more appropriate for 'a Burgher's near to a great town, than for a Gentleman's seat in the Country'.

Bobbing John countered with a grandiose scheme, incorporating a tree-lined canal 1,000 yards long. This proved too much even for the dutiful Lord Dun, though William Adam – who was finally brought in, possibly at Lord Mar's own suggestion – did borrow Bobbing John's idea of a monumental niche on the entrance front. This can be seen at the centre of the implied triumphal arch which gives the House of Dun its special character.

Adam appears to have based his design on the Chateau d'Issy, near Paris, which was built by the French architect Pierre Bullet for the Princesse de Conti. This building was very familiar to Lord Mar who encouraged Adam to tickle up his original design of 1730 to make it more ornamental. As it turned out, the intended balustrades and urn finials on the north and south fronts were not executed but, in an admirably bold move, the National Trust for Scotland has recently created and installed them, based on Adam's designs.

Majestic as the unusual exterior undoubtedly is, the highpoint of the House of Dun has to be the glorious plasterwork in the Saloon by Enzer, who also worked for William Adam at Arniston and Yester (qqv). One stands there quite overwhelmed by the sheer swagger of the assorted chunky trophies, armour and classical figures. What they all signify has exercised the experts. John Cornforth has suggested that the Mars overmantel seems to be inspired by a military trophy at the Dutch royal palace of Het Loo by Daniel Marot (which also influenced Thomas Clayton's work at Blair Castle – qv) but some of the other features, such as a stag hunt bizarrely caught up with cherubs frolicking in the briny, defy rational explanation. William Kay of St Andrews University has detected some obscure Jacobite symbolism in the decoration, of which doubtless Bobbing John would have approved.

Enzer was paid £216 for a year's work as late as 1742 – an indication that progress on the new House of Dun was not particularly swift, though his flour-ishes seem to have been the final touches to the project. Subsequent Lairds tended to concentrate on agriculture and sport, none more so than the spinster

PRECEDING PAGES Detail of Joseph Enzer's plasterwork in the Saloon, showing a watchful Scottish lion.

RIGHT A bas-relief of Mars dominates the far wall of the Saloon. The Roman god of war stands 'guardant' above the Scottish regalia.

BELOW A triton blows a conch-shell at the front of Neptune's chariot drawn by *hippocampi*, or web-footed sea horses. The aquatic theme possibly alludes to 'the King over the water'.

Martial doorway in the Saloon.

William Adam's 'withdrawing room' which was given a colonnaded screen and enlarged into the present Dining Room in the early 19th century. The furniture was supplied by the Edinburgh cabinet-maker William Trotter in 1828. The marble chimneypiece is original William Adam.

16th Laird, Alice Erskine, a woman of masculine habits who was prone to crashing around the country on her sturdy hunter with her ill-fitting red wig askew. She would usually be accompanied by a faithful old retainer, who had lost a hand in a shooting accident, brandishing a hook.

Alice slept in a bedroom overlooking the stableyard so that she could bellow down to the stable lads and also oversee the duties of the henwife in the Hen House (which is happily extant with its original 18th-century nesting boxes). She turned the old formal garden to the east into an exercise ground for her horses. Rather surprisingly, though, according to the building accounts of the time, Alice also seems to have carried out some architectural alterations inside the house.

More significant modernization was to be undertaken by her nephew, John Kennedy-Erskine (younger brother of the 2nd Marquess of Ailsa, of Culzean – *qv*) and his wife, Lady Augusta. They opened up the hall with an arch (described as 'rather slack' by Cornforth) leading to the staircase and dismantled Lord Dun's library, which had occupied the big room over the Saloon. Lady Augusta, who lived on at the House of Dun for another 34 years after her husband's death in 1831, was a passionate botanist and gardener. In her bright yellow carriage drawn by two dapple-grey horses, she would scour the surrounding countryside on the lookout for wild specimens.

The carriage and the horses, as well as the coachman (and a splendid mahogany four-poster bed now to be seen in the Red Bedroom), were wedding presents from her father, King William IV. For Lady Augusta was one of the bluff old 'Sailor King's' ten natural children by the actress Mrs Jordan – a liaison popularly described as 'bathing in the River Jordan'.

Lady Augusta turned Alice's old equestrian exercise ground into a flower garden, laid out the terraces and yew hedging on the south side of the house looking out to the Montrose Basin and created some ravishing woodland walks. She was also an accomplished needlewoman, though she would depute the tedious background work to her French chef.

The third of Dun's remarkable trio of women was Lady Augusta's granddaughter, the author and artist Violet Jacob, celebrated for her poem *The Sheep Stealers*. Like her grandmother, Violet was an ardent botanist and painted

ABOVE View from Saloon into Entrance Hall.

LEFT The Entrance Hall, with more plasterwork by Enzer. The busts are (*left*) Rear-Admiral Adolphus FitzClarence (by Samuel Joseph, 1854), a favourite brother of Lady Augusta, the châtelaine of Dun, and (*right*) Lady Augusta's son, William Henry Kennedy-Erskine, the 18th Laird (by C.E. Fuller, 1857).

numerous indigenous wild flowers during her time in India as the wife of an officer in the 20th Hussars. She was haunted by her memories of the House of Dun: 'The trees that shelter it on three sides give it a tremendous solemnity, and the associations that brood like a cloud of witnesses about it seem as much part of its life as the coming and going of latter-day feet.'

As the 20th century progressed, these brooding clouds came to dominate the House of Dun. The house was unsympathetically altered in 1912. Subsequently the 20th Laird ended his days in a psychiatric hospital and his spinster sister, Marjorie, committed suicide believing herself – according to the inquest – to be under the spell of a dealer in Black Magic. Their sister, Millicent Lovett, the 21st Laird, let out the House of Dun as a sporting hotel. William Adam's Parlour, which had been used as a smoking room in the 19th century, found itself called 'The Whips Bar'.

Finally, in 1980, Millicent Lovett, the last Laird, died and bequeathed the estate, house and contents to the National Trust for Scotland. The Trust's expert team of David Learmont, Christopher Hartley and John Batty did a marvellous job of restoring the place without turning it into a museum. The rooms, both 'upstairs' and 'downstairs', are full of vitality and character. The Saloon has sensibly been made an uncluttered room of parade; the Dining Room hung with family portraits; the 'Whips Bar' ingeniously converted back to the Parlour; the Library re-created. Especially atmospheric are the Gun and Rod Rooms in the basement – gamily evocative of the Edwardian Laird and his sport – and the Kitchen, complete with copper *batterie de cuisine*.

Queen Elizabeth The Queen Mother, the National Trust for Scotland's Patron, came to tea at the House of Dun in May 1989 when she officially opened it to the public. Many visitors since have delighted in both the Trust's sensitive and unstuffy restoration of a fascinating architectural gem and the feeling nicely expressed by John Cornforth that 'they can imagine themselves on a visit to an elderly uncle or aunt, with solid meals in the dining room, a loyal but invisible staff and pleasurable fishing expeditions'.

The entrance front, with the south bank of the Montrose Basin in the background.

17

HADDO HOUSE

ABERDEENSHIRE

O NE OF the hardest problems for any National Trust, or similar body today, when preserving a country house is to avoid 'museumization'. As we have seen in the previous chapter, on the House of Dun (*qv*), it can be done, but it is assuredly much easier to achieve when the donor family is still in residence. This is happily still the case at Haddo House, near Aberdeen, where June Marchioness of Aberdeen, widow of the 4th Marquess of Aberdeen and Temair (who made over the property to the NTS shortly before his death in 1974) and a legendary live-wire personality in her own right, ensures that the place retains a strong family atmosphere.

The daughter of a brilliant Headmaster of Harrow – where the Gordons, Earls and Marquesses of Aberdeen, have been educated for generations – the former June Boissier is a trained musician and a passionate champion of the arts. Together with her husband, David, the 4th Marquess, she developed the Haddo House Choral Society from small beginnings, as his brainchild, to become one of Scotland's major cultural ventures. Haddo has earned a reputation as a thriving centre for artistic endeavours; operas have been staged as well as seasons of plays, some of them starring Prince Edward. Photographs of visiting eminences and artistes who have performed here – from Ralph Vaughan Williams and Sir Adrian Boult to modern television personalities – enliven the Drawing Room.

Many of these famous visitors have become close friends. One recalled of the 4th Marquess and his wife:

> The great house was wide open, like their hearts, to every sort and
> kind of friend. And their friends became friends of each other in
> that special warmth. David combined huge strength with huge
> gentleness, great possessions with great generosity. These gifts, in
> partnership with his wife's creative talent, made Haddo not so
> much a place as an experience.

– 175 –

The building of the original Haddo House in the 1730s must have proved no less of an experience, even a shock, to the hardy folk of the Grampians used to bleak castles and tower-houses in these rugged north-eastern parts rather than elegant exercises in the Palladian manner. Hitherto the Gordons of Haddo (an estate acquired in 1469 from the Foulartons) had been content to live in the old 'Place of Kellie', though, according to one 17th-century account, this was no spartan affair but a sumptuously furnished house.

In any event, it was set on fire and the surrounding country laid waste in 1645 after Sir John Gordon, 1st Bt, of Haddo (a staunch Royalist who had served as second-in-command to his kinsman, the 2nd Marquess of Huntly, 'Cock o' the North', who was eventually beheaded after a long imprisonment) had been besieged by the Covenanters under the 1st Marquess of Argyll. Sir John was locked up in St Giles Cathedral in Edinburgh (where his cell, a recess in the wall, became known as 'Haddo's Hole') before being executed. He thus became the first Royalist to suffer death by judicial sentence and – as the patent creating his younger son, George, Earl of Aberdeen in 1682 noted – 'he died a martyr for us and our Crown'.

ABOVE The comfortable Drawing Room, which retains its 1880 decorative scheme. The chandelier and most of the furniture were supplied by Wright & Mansfield. Above the fireplace is Domenichino's study of David, the slayer of Goliath. When the 1st Marquess of Aberdeen's wife was taking a party round Haddo, her enquiry as to who they thought the figure might be was answered by one bemused visitor with 'Could it be your Ladyship?'

ABOVE RIGHT The even cosier Morning Room, also redecorated in the 1880s during the reign of 'We Twa' (as the 1st Marquess and his wife, the former Ishbel Marjoribanks, called themselves). Previously, in the time of the 4th Earl of Aberdeen, it had become a library. The watercolours are by James Giles (the Aberdeenshire artist who helped the 4th Earl lay out the grounds) and by the female half of 'We Twa' herself.

PRECEDING PAGES The curved corridor, lined with busts, which links the main block of Haddo to the north wing.

ABOVE Detail of neo-Classical decoration and service bell in Morning Room.

George, despite being Lord High Chancellor of Scotland and making a prosperous marriage to a Lockhart heiress, did not see the need to build a new pile for himself and died at the (presumably repaired) Kellie in 1720. His son and successor, William, the 2nd Earl of Aberdeen, had grander ideas. According to the witty account of the family in *A Wild Flight of Gordons* by Archie Gordon (otherwise the bachelor 5th Marquess of Aberdeen, author and radio producer, whose startling modern portrait by Maggie Hambling is one of the most vibrant surprises in the house), the 2nd Earl was 'ambitious, financially accumulative and a thumping snob'.

Besides marrying first the daughter of an Earl (Leven and Melville) and then the daughters of two Dukes (Atholl and Gordon), William expanded the estates considerably and consulted Sir John Clerk of Penicuik, the Palladian pundit and friend of the architect Earl of Burlington, about creating a suitable new seat. Clerk, whose poem *The Country Seat* (1727) set out the rules of the game, recommended the services of William Adam (who else?) as architect and John Baxter, who had just finished work on Clerk's own villa of Mavisbank, as the mason to supervise the building work.

They did not hang around. First of all, Baxter demolished the old house of Kellie in the spring of 1732 and by that autumn the new building, on the same site, was as high as the second storey despite using 'white asheller all wrought wt. hammers which is a longesom work'. A year later, the house was 'now near Roffed' with timber from Norway. By 1734 one of the two flanking pavilions and the curved corridor to the central block was 'joiste high'; by 1735 the second wing was completed. The house, observed the efficient Baxter, 'stanes well without crack or flau or the least simptem of a sitle in any pairt of the whoall'.

Unfortunately, the 2nd Earl of Aberdeen's successor, 'the Wicked Earl', did not greatly care for his father's spanking new house and preferred to expend his not inconsiderable energies elsewhere. Archie Gordon pithily sums him up: 'He neglected Haddo House and its châtelaine, loved his extra-marital families, especially those at Ellon [a castle not far from Haddo], was very smart at the business of making his estates pay for his heavy commitments, and referred to himself as "us".'

ABOVE Rounding the corner *en route* for the Library.

RIGHT The Library, another splendid room of the 1880s (converted from haylofts over the stables), with cedar woodwork inlaid with ebony. The marble chimneypiece contains copies of Wedgwood jasperware plaques taken from an original in Brook House.

The châtelaine he neglected was a former cook at a Yorkshire inn – where the Wicked Earl put up in 1759. The story goes that he so enjoyed the mutton chops there that he insisted on complimenting the tender of the stove in person – whom he found no less succulent. On his next visit the doughty cook, brandishing pistols, demanded marriage or his life.

The Wicked Earl also neglected the education of his eventual heir, George, who was left orphaned and virtually penniless by the early deaths of his parents, Lord and Lady Haddo, in the 1790s. Being an enterprising lad, though, young George, stranded in London, enlisted the help of a fellow Scot, Viscount Melville (of the Dundas dynasty of Arniston – *qv*). No less a personage than the Prime Minister, William Pitt, also agreed to act as one of the boy's curators and memorably reproved the Wicked Earl for his negligence, with the dry observation that he 'did not concur with his Lordship in considering that rank superseded the necessity for education'.

George was duly sent to Harrow and Cambridge where he distinguished himself as a Classical scholar. Subsequently, as *The Complete Peerage* puts it, he 'travelled far in the bypaths of literature' and the poet Lord Byron (a kinsman and fellow Harrovian) sang of him in *English Bards and Scotch Reviews* as 'the travelled thane, Athenian Aberdeen'. An upright and cultured figure, Athenian Aberdeen soon made his mark in politics and after stints as Foreign and Colonial Secretary became Prime Minister himself in 1852. Three years later he had to resign after the Coalition he led was blamed for the mismanagement of the Crimean War; but, as *The Times* obituary was to point out, Lord Aberdeen 'belonged to that class of statesman who are great without being brilliant, who succeed without ambition, who without eloquence become famous, who retain their power even when deprived of place'.

As for his own place in the country, Haddo House, the 4th Earl carried out some significant changes early in the 19th century. The Aberdeen architect Archibald Simpson was commissioned to raise by a storey the curved corridors which join the central block to the wings. The southern wing (which housed the kitchens and domestic offices) was enlarged around an office court, terminating in a clock tower with cupola.

Outside, the 4th Earl laid out a grass terrace and a double lime avenue beyond it, to the east, and employed James Giles, the local landscape artist, to supervise

The entrance front.

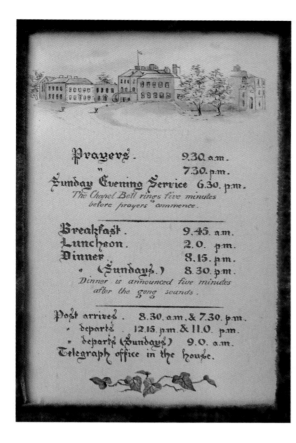

ABOVE Order of the day: prayers take precedence.

BELOW The east window of G.E. Street's Chapel of 1881; the upper lights are by the architect's pupil, Edward Burne-Jones.

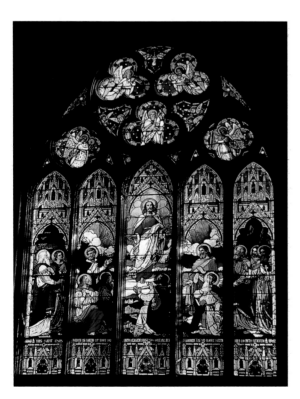

the planting of thousands of trees and the formation of a chain of three lakes in the park. To celebrate his installation as a Knight of the Garter in 1855 – a singular honour for a Scotsman who was also a Knight of the Thistle – he inserted an elaborate armorial panel above the central Drawing Room window which led to the terrace. Queen Victoria, who had granted him the very rare distinction of being permitted to retain the Thistle as well as the Garter, came to stay at Haddo two years later.

Athenian Aberdeen's eldest son, the 5th Earl, was dogged by ill health and spent much of his time in Egypt, where he and his wife (a Baillie of Mellerstain – *qv*) would distribute Christian pamphlets to the natives as they sailed up and down the Nile. Their eldest son, the 6th Earl, went in for sailing of a more rigorous kind after he ran away to sea in 1866 on finding his inheritance too much of a worry. Under the pseudonym of 'George Osborne' he worked as an ordinary seaman before the mast in the United States Mercantile Marine. His family never saw him again. Four years later, having sailed in many different vessels and obtained his captain's certificate through his own hard work, he was dragged overboard by a rope and drowned while *en route* for Australia. He left behind a reputation, among his former shipmates, for great goodness and integrity.

And so Haddo and the estates of some 75,000 acres passed to his younger brother, the 7th Earl of Aberdeen, who had a long and distinguished public career, serving as Governor-General of Canada and Viceroy of Ireland and being promoted to a Marquessate. His formidable wife, Ishbel Marjoribanks, was not initially impressed by Haddo – 'Why have you brought me to this horrible house?' she enquired of her husband – and promptly set about a radical programme of improvements which largely shaped the house we see today. The south wing was converted into family rooms; a beautifully austere Gothic chapel was built to the designs of G.E. Street (of London Law Courts fame); and the Edinburgh architects, Wardrop & Reid, created a new ground-floor entrance hall and associated staircases on the west front. This spoilt the Palladian purity of the principal elevation, though it undoubtedly enhanced Haddo's comfortable atmosphere. Wardrop & Reid also built the Community Hall, scene of so much artistic activity in recent years.

The 1st Marquess of Aberdeen and his wife liked referring to themselves as 'We Twa' (indeed they published two volumes entitled *We Twa* and *More Cracks with We Twa*), rather in the way the Wicked Earl called himself 'us'. There was, though, nothing wicked about We Twa, who devoted themselves to philanthropic and charitable works. Lady Aberdeen's numerous appointments included the presidency of the International Council of Women and she founded the Onward and Upward Association for the betterment of servant girls.

We Twa's good works had a deleterious effect on the family fortunes and it took much effort by the 2nd and 4th Marquesses to maintain the greatly reduced estate (it had shrunk by two-thirds at the time of the 1st Marquess's death in 1934). Fortunately the 4th Marquess, who took over the running of the estate at the end of the Second World War (when Haddo was a maternity home), was a trained land agent and a far-sighted polymath who secured the house's future by arranging for it to be cared for by the National Trust for Scotland. His dynamic widow, June, continues to live in the family wing (gutted by fire in 1930 and sensibly rebuilt by Bennett Mitchell & Son of Aberdeen for the 2nd Marquess), whereas the estate is now owned by their nephew, the Earl of Haddo, son and heir of the 6th Marquess of Aberdeen and Temair, an artist specializing in flower painting from his home in Berkshire.

18

DUFF
HOUSE

B Y THE 1970s, art galleries, caught in the vice-like grip of the 'Modern' Movement, had become deeply depressing affairs. Historic pictures, many of which had once hung in great country houses, were unimaginatively displayed under strip-lights on stark walls (sometimes adorned with hessian) in soulless spaces dotted with the occasional 'leatherette' bench. Much of the credit for the transformation of such dreary and anti-historical interiors into vibrant and aesthetically appropriate settings for works of art must go to the enthusiastic Tim Clifford, who made his mark as director of the Manchester City Galleries from the late 1970s before being appointed director of the National Galleries of Scotland in 1984.

As well as breathing new life into the main galleries in Edinburgh, which suddenly became full of vigour with pictures hung as they would be in a family house against a robust background of richly coloured walls and surrounded by furniture and *objets d'art* which delighted the eye, Clifford also encouraged the setting-up of 'outstations', whereby parts of the national collections could be shown in country houses. These have included the sumptuous Regency gallery at Paxton House, on the Tweed, the family seat of the Home Robertsons which is now vested in a charitable trust set up with the help of the National Heritage Memorial Fund. The premier 'outstation', though, is undoubtedly Duff House – an astonishing and hitherto all too little-known Baroque pile wedged between two small seaside towns, Macduff and Banff, in one of north-east Scotland's dimmest counties.

Some ten years ago Duff was, to say the least, a 'problem' house. In the course of the 20th century this former treasure-house of the Duffs, Earls and Dukes of Fife, had suffered the indignities of being variously a sanatorium for sufferers from habitual constipation ('disorders of nutrition, excluding inebriation', as the brochure tactfully put it), a prisoner-of-war camp and a troops billet. In 1956 the Ministry of Works, concerned at the fate of 'this fine example of architecture

– 183 –

in the grand manner', took Duff under its wing and carried out essential repairs. It was even opened to the public on a very limited scale; Tim Clifford recalls that only two rooms were decorated – 'There were four family portraits of the former owners on display, but otherwise it was populated by a seatter of art-paper white mannequins, like ghosts, seated in the principal rooms.'

What was to be done? In 1988 the official organization then responsible for Duff, Historic Buildings and Monuments (later to become 'Historic Scotland'), called a public meeting to try to find a suitable role for the house. This was attended by representatives from all the conservation bodies in Scotland, and eventually, at a second meeting, the enterprising Tim Clifford and the National Galleries came up with a solution to the problem. The proposal was that if running costs could be secured locally, and if the building were to be properly restored and suitably equipped for museum purposes, the National Galleries would not only provide pictures for the house but also endeavour to find suitable furnishings.

The old official guide-book of 1985 may have lamented that 'the rich profusion of furnishings and paintings is beyond recall' but Tim Clifford argued that filling the house once more with appropriate furnishings and pictures could help us 'imagine more clearly the former function and spirit of a remarkable house'. Happily, his passionate and practical scheme won the day and in the 1990s, thanks to an unprecedented partnership between Historic Scotland (which contributed £2 million to the restoration of the fabric), the National Galleries of Scotland, Grampian Regional Council, Banff and Buchan District Council, and with assistance from Grampian Enterprise Ltd, Duff was indeed restored to much of its former glory.

Nearly all the pictures now hanging at Duff House were sought out from the National Galleries' own reserves. 'The pictures,' explains Tim Clifford, 'have not been chosen for their "star" quality – although there are many stars amongst them – but to furnish appropriately a great aristocratic country house.' Quite rightly, Clifford makes no apology for the preponderance of portraits, because that is what has always hung here. Nor is he impressed by criticism of the dense picture-hanging arrangements, for this again closely follows the pattern of how the house must have looked in its heyday.

Indeed in that heyday, the late 18th century, Duff was not so dissimilar to the country-house gallery it has become today. For the 2nd Earl Fife, a

PRECEDING PAGES The south (entrance) front; William Adam's planned wings and quadrant colonnades were never built.

ABOVE Roof view of the bridge over the River Deveron, the fishing village of Macduff and the sea.

LEFT The Vestibule, dominated by William Etty's *The Combat, Women Pleading for the Vanquished – an ideal groupe* (exhibited at the Royal Academy in 1825). According to the artist, the picture symbolizes the Beauty of Mercy.

RIGHT View through to the Great Staircase from the Vestibule.

LEFT The Dining Room, a handsome interior of
the 1750s, with a *papier-mâché* ceiling installed
for the 2nd Earl Fife in 1761. The mahogany
table came from Dunimarle, Fife; the gilt-
bronzed candelabra are after a design by C.H.
Tatham (1801) and were made by Storr &
Mortimer for the 4th Earl Fife.

BELOW *Mrs Daniel Cunyngham*: an early
portrait by Allan Ramsay, and one of the finest
pictures at Duff. The magnificent Rococo frame
is original.

Fellow of both the Royal Society and the Society of Antiquaries, was a celebrated connoisseur and a pioneer collector of portraits on historical lines. The upper rooms at Duff were completed in the 1790s in order to display his ever-expanding picture collection.

The 2nd Earl, who sat as the local MP (the earldom was in the Peerage of Ireland and did not provide a seat in the Lords), was a shrewd businessman and, as *Burke's Peerage* noted, 'by judicious purchases he nearly doubled the possessions of his family'. He created a harbour at the local town of Doune which he managed to have made into a 'burgh' duly renamed Macduff.

The Duff coffers were already well-lined. The 2nd Earl's grandfather, William Duff of Dipple, left his eldest son and namesake estates with a rental of £8,500 a year on his death in 1722 – in those days the largest fortune in the north of Scotland. Young William added considerably to the family land-holdings and was created a peer of Ireland (a convenient device often deployed for politicians with not the slightest Irish connection) as Lord Braco in 1735. In the same year, having retired as MP for Banffshire, he embarked on the build-ing of Duff House to the designs of William Adam.

Previously Lord Braco had toyed with the idea of altering and enlarging the old house in Banff town, but Adam's gloriously ambitious scheme for a great Classical palace demanded a virgin site. The design of Duff has prompted John Cornforth of *Country Life* to enthuse about 'echoes of Castle Howard and surely of Houghton, too; of Hawksmoor, particularly at Easton Neston; and of Gibbs, in its plan and ornaments'. Gibbs had provided the designs for Lord Braco's earlier adventure in architecture, Balvenie, an austere Classical house near Dufftown.

Yet the wonderfully flamboyant Duff could, as Cornforth says, 'only be a Scottish building, in its height, strength and upward thrust'. An instructive model on show at Duff (made by Simon Montgomery in 1989) shows that Adam's original intention was to set off the towering central block with quadrant colonnades and two flanking wings. This was to be the Duff family's triumphant expression of their magnate status.

In the event, the wings were never built, and the fitting-up of the interior was abandoned after a corking row between patron and architect ended up in the Law Courts. To the fury of the 1st Earl Fife (as Lord Braco became in 1739 when the shell of the house was complete) William Adam overcharged for the stonemasons' work and the architect was obliged to sue for parts of his costs. The atmosphere at Duff was not improved by the conflict between the 1st Earl, a staunch supporter of the Hanoverian Government, and his Jacobite elder son, another William – who, doubtless to his father's satisfaction, predeceased him as a bachelor in 1753.

The completion of the interior was left to the 2nd Earl Fife. First, in the late 1750s, came the first floor (always intended to be for daily living). The Dining Room is a particularly pleasing example from this period of decoration, with its carved panelling, pilasters and a *papier-mâché* ceiling. Then, in the 1780s, the 2nd Earl constructed the main staircase before completing the two big rooms on the second floor (planned by Adam for State).

Further redecoration was carried out by the 4th Earl Fife, a former Major-General in the Spanish Army who had fought with the future Duke of Wellington in the Peninsular War and was another collector of pictures. John Jackson's stencil painting in the Vestibule and Great Staircase dates from the 4th Earl's time.

The last principal stage of decoration was done by the wife of the 5th Earl, the former Lady Agnes Hay, in the 1860s before she died as a result of

Stairwell.

LEFT The Great Staircase.

RIGHT The North Drawing Room, notable for its sumptuous suite of gilded furniture (complete with original case covers in blue linen damask and crimson piping) from the collection of Cardinal Fesch, Archbishop of Paris and Lyons, who is said to have been given the pieces by his step-nephew, the Emperor Napoleon.

a fall from her carriage. It was she who enriched the North Drawing Room and added gilding to some of the other interiors. Lady Agnes's mother, Lady Elizabeth FitzClarence was an illegitimate daughter of King William IV and later in the 19th century Duff acquired an even stronger royal connection when Lady Agnes's son, the 6th Earl Fife, married Princess Louise, the future Princess Royal, eldest daughter of the Prince of Wales (later King Edward VII), who stayed at Duff in 1883. Two days after the wedding, in July 1889, Queen Victoria created her grandson-in-law Duke of Fife.

Although David Bryce had added a new kitchen and bedroom wing in 1870 for the 5th Earl, Duff proved less appealing to the new royal châtelaine than a rebuilt Mar Lodge close to Balmoral. And so in 1906 the Duke of Fife, by then in financial difficulties, presented Duff House, plus 140 acres, to the burgh of Banff and one of William Adam's greatest architectural achievements rather disappeared from view.

Today, though, it has bounced back into life. As well as the splendid architecture, with the turret-like pavilions and facades richly ornamented by pilasters, pediments and urns, one can enjoy a feast of good pictures (such as El Greco's *St Jerome in Penitence*, J.G. Cuyp's Dutch family group, panels by François Boucher and portraits dominated by Allan Ramsay's full-length study of *Mrs Daniel Cunyngham*) and some magnificent furniture. Especially impressive are the suites said to have been given by Napoleon to his step-uncle, Cardinal Fesch, which are on loan from the Magdalene Sharpe Erskine Trust of Dunimarle, Culross, Fife. The Marquess of Zetland has lent a superb suite of furniture made by Thomas Chippendale to the design of Robert Adam.

The new Duff House only opened its doors in 1995 and, as Tim Clifford says, these are still early days in the long campaign to furnish it completely. Yet already plenty of visitors are bringing back excited reports that Duff is a delightful discovery, reflecting a new dawn in the intelligent celebration of the country house as a lively temple of the arts.

19

INVERARAY CASTLE

ARGYLL

THE FAMILY seat of the Campbells, Dukes of Argyll, nicely encapsulates their role in developing the Western Highlands and Islands for the British Crown without losing faith with the essential Scottish spirit embodied in the proud title of *Mac Cailein Mor*, Chief of the Clan. For while Inveraray Castle was designed by an English architect (the Palladian Roger Morris) and neatly placed in an idealized and reclaimed landscape, complete with model town, its rugged mountainous setting beside the haunting waters of Loch Fyne is inescapably Gaelic.

Indeed the family history of the Campbells is effectively the history of Scotland. The Duke of Argyll is one of the few Highland Chiefs in the old Peerage of Scotland. His ancestors became Earls in the 15th century, when they moved their headquarters from the fresh-water of Loch Awe to the seawater of Loch Fyne; rising to a Marquessate in the 17th century, when the 1st (and only) Marquess abandoned the traditional Campbell loyalty to the Stuarts and led the Covenanters in the Civil War; and finally to a Dukedom in 1701, when King William III rewarded his faithful lieutenant in the 'Glorious Revolution'.

The 2nd Duke of Argyll, one of the first two Field Marshals to be created in the British Army, followed his father in being a staunch anti-Jacobite. Not long after the first Rising – or 'Rebellion', as he, the victor of Sheriffmuir, would have described it – the 2nd Duke considered a grandiose scheme by Sir John Vanbrugh of Blenheim and Castle Howard fame to build a new castle on the bank of the Aray. The 15th-century tower-house there was crumbling away and the Duke, who, according to Horace Walpole in an otherwise unflattering profile, had 'a head admirably turned to mechanics', must have been tempted. In the event, though, he preferred to pursue his passion for planting in England; it was left to his brother, Archibald, to start the great project.

Duke Archibald did not come into the estates until 1743 when he was 61. Yet nothing – not even Inveraray's extraordinary remoteness at that time

PRECEDING PAGES The garden front of the castle.

LEFT The Saloon: appliqués gilded by Maitland Bogg of Edinburgh (1788); Thomas Gainsborough's portrait of Field Marshal Henry Seymour-Conway, Secretary of State for the Northern Department and son-in-law of the 4th Duke of Argyll; and sofa gilded by Dupasquier (1782).

RIGHT The stupendous Armoury Hall, devised by Anthony Salvin after the fire of 1877 and recently repainted.

– was going to stop him from realizing the dream of creating not only a new castle but a new setting too. The old town that abutted the old castle was to be swept away and rebuilt on a new site, the surrounding land transformed into a nobleman's park.

The new castle, adapted by Morris from the original sketch by Vanbrugh (with whom he had worked at Eastbury Park in Dorset) and tricked up with the newly fashionable Gothick ornament, was intended to contrast its symmetry against the wildness of the landscape. Morris had come into the Argylls' ken through his work for the Board of Ordnance. Although the architect was seldom able to visit the site, William Adam kept an eye on the building operations and work proceeded as best it could considering the handicaps of transport and such local difficulties as the 1745 Jacobite Rising. The walls and roof were up within ten years and the structure was completed in 1758.

Unfortunately Duke Archibald was never able to occupy the new castle. By the time Dr Johnson came to Inveraray in 1773, though, it was fully occupied, with the 5th Duke of Argyll, another Field Marshal, and his family comfortably installed. His wife Elizabeth, a celebrated beauty of the Court of King George III, was one of the three Gunning sisters from Co. Roscommon. Their looks were so famous that on one occasion, when the Gunning girls

LEFT The Tapestry Drawing Room: a touch of Paris in the Highlands. The Beauvais tapestries, known as *Pastorales à draperies bleues et arabesques* (after J.B. Huet), are thought to be the only 18th-century set still in the room for which they were made. The Inveraray set was commissioned by the 5th Duke of Argyll in 1785 and hung two years later.

RIGHT Detail of a caryatid supporting the marble chimneypiece of 1800 in the Tapestry Drawing Room.

were passing through Doncaster, the street was full of an admiring crowd at early dawn to see them start for the North. Elizabeth's first husband was the 6th Duke of Hamilton and her subsequent marriage to another Duke moved Horace Walpole to raptures: 'A match that would not disgrace Arcadia…they reconcile contending clans.' This 'picture of majestic modesty' (portrayed by Allan Ramsay) treated Dr Johnson kindly, though studiously ignored his travelling companion, James Boswell.

Dr Johnson was impressed enough by the unusual slate-like stone (from Creggans, on the other side of Loch Fyne) of the castle but felt it would look better if raised by an additional storey. The 5th Duke, though, had his own ideas for improvements. Robert Mylne, scion of a remarkable dynasty of master masons who had been employed by the Kings of Scots since the 15th century, was brought in to re-cast the interiors in the 1780s. The windows were lengthened to reach floor level and the main entrance was switched from the south to the north, where a former gallery was divided up into an entrance hall (with a Gothic ceiling) and rooms either side.

The Dining Room and the Drawing Room were redecorated in a French style made newly fashionable by the Prince of Wales (the future King George IV) at Carlton House in London. The Prince's exquisite creation did not survive for long so this makes the Inveraray interiors all the more important, though 'important' seems far too dull a word to describe such gay and ravishing confections with their *grisailles* by Guinand and floral ornamentation by Girard (who worked at Carlton House). The architectural historian Colin McWilliam considered the Dining Room 'perhaps the finest painted room in Britain', and it would be hard to disagree. Its delicate arabesques and figures would, as he said, 'not look out of place at Bagatelle or Fontainebleau'. The Drawing Room is adorned with seven Beauvais tapestries from the *Pastorales* set, woven after designs by Huet.

Robert Mylne also busied himself outside the castle: he was responsible for designing the stable quadrangle, known as Cherry Park, the Aray Bridge, and much of the model new town (the first of its kind in Scotland), including the church. The 5th Duke of Argyll tended to devote his energies to improving the town rather than the castle after his beloved Duchess Elizabeth died in 1790.

In the 19th century Dr Johnson's wish for Inveraray was partly fulfilled, as the result of a disastrous fire in 1877. The upper floors were gutted and as

a consequence the battlements were removed and dormer windows superimposed. To make those changes the 8th Duke of Argyll, a prominent Liberal politician whose Government positions included Lord Privy Seal and Secretary of State for India, consulted Anthony Salvin, the Victorian castle specialist, who could not resist adding the jolly conical roofs on the corner towers.

Although the State rooms escaped the fire of 1877, the central tower was gutted and Salvin redesigned it as an Armoury Hall. The displays of weaponry, fantastically piled in wheels and fans, includes 'Brown Bess' muskets that were used in the '45 Rising, Lochaber axes and fearsome Highland broadswords. The arms stretching upwards in the 70-foot-high tower make an astonishing impact on the visitor.

Shortly before the fire, the 8th Duke of Argyll's eldest son and heir, the Marquess of Lorne, strengthened the family's close links to the Crown by marrying Princess Louise, Queen Victoria's fourth – and most beautiful – daughter. Queen Victoria, with her love of all things Scots, approved of the union, though some of her stuffier German cousins took a dim view of a match between a sovereign's daughter and a subject.

ABOVE The State Dining Room: perhaps the finest painted room in Britain. The French decorative painters were Girard and Guinand, whose work only survives at Inveraray. The chandelier is Waterford, *circa* 1830; the silver-gilt *nefs*, or sailing ships are German, *circa* 1900. The portrait over the fireplace is of the 4th Duke of Argyll, in his Coronation robes.

RIGHT Detail of painted panels.

The Victoria Room at Inveraray contains the maplewood writing desk given by Queen Victoria to Princess Louise (who became a talented sculptress) on her marriage in 1871. The occasion was marked at the castle by the construction of an elaborate glass and iron-covered entrance bridge to the design of Matthew Digby Wyatt, one of the well-known English architectural dynasty who had already done this kind of work on a somewhat larger scale at Paddington Station in London. In the early 1890s Inveraray became the first house to be installed with electricity in Scotland.

Lord Lorne, who became the 9th Duke of Argyll, died childless and his successor, the 10th Duke, was a bachelor so Inveraray remained virtually untouched for the first half of the 20th century. Then, with the help of the distinguished architect Ian Lindsay (who was to write a masterly history of *Inveraray and the Dukes of Argyll* in collaboration with Mary Cosh), the 11th Duke carried out a sympathetic restoration of both the castle and the town. The castle had fallen prey to dry and wet rot and had to be rewired, re-roofed, re-floored, re-fenestrated and comprehensively repaired before it could be opened to the public in 1953.

Shortly after the present Duke of Argyll succeeded to Inveraray 20 years later, though, disaster struck again. Another fire, nearly a century on from the previous one, broke out in November 1975. The castle was gutted in the conflagration, but admirably swift action managed to save the State rooms once more, and most of the contents. With great determination and drive, the present Duke and his Duchess, formerly Miss Iona Colquhoun of Luss, set about making good the damage. The building was repaired with remarkable dispatch, the painted rooms restored, the tapestries cleaned.

Recently, some 20 years on, the Duke and Duchess decided that their efforts, while effective in the short term after the 1975 disaster, had not, in the words of the Duke, been 'as permanent as those carried out by the 5th Duke in 1785'. Accordingly they embarked upon a mammoth project of their own, involving some 20 tonnes of scaffolding in the central towers. All the arms, pictures

ABOVE Bird's-eye view of town and castle.

LEFT The model town of Inveraray on the shores of Loch Fyne.

and tapestries came down and went into store while the conservation team devoted themselves to relining, pointing and plastering, as well as painting, the house in the authentic 18th-century manner.

We arrived to find everything looking in absolutely spanking condition. Surely in its long history Inveraray has never looked better – a fitting showplace for the headquarters of the Clan Campbell and the epitome of the Anglo–Scottish experience at its best.

20

CULZEAN CASTLE

AYRSHIRE

T HE SEA, the sea ... Of all the great houses of Scotland benefiting from a maritime position, none can match Culzean Castle, perched on a clifftop above the Ayrshire coastline, for sheer spectacle and drama. Robert Adam's romantic creation for the Kennedys, Earls of Cassillis (and later Marquesses of Ailsa), now the flagship property of the National Trust for Scotland, enjoys views that are without rival in Europe. You look out from the windows and battlements of the 18th-century castle across the Firth of Clyde to the mountains of Arran, while to the left the brooding Ailsa Craig, a rocky island rising to 1,114 feet, looms out of the sea.

The Kennedy family had been seated hereabouts since medieval times, Culzean being only one of a dozen small castles in their hands as they rose to be the most prominent landowning dynasty in Ayrshire. The family history is typically chock-a-block with battles, bloodshed, feuds and poisoning. The 1st Earl of Cassillis fell at Flodden; the 2nd Earl was murdered; the 3rd Earl was poisoned at Dieppe after helping to negotiate the marriage of the infant Mary Queen of Scots to the Dauphin of France. The 4th Earl, notorious for roasting the wretched Commendator of Crossraguel Abbey after that worthy declined to hand over Abbey lands to the Kennedys, died after a fall from his horse.

The 4th Earl of Cassillis's brother, Sir Thomas Kennedy of Culzean (murdered on the Sands of Ayr in 1602), was the ancestor of the line of Kennedys that were to improve and extend the castle. Originally it was a comparatively modest Scots tower-house, with an L-shaped tower, vaulted service quarters on the ground floor, a single great hall occupying the whole of the first floor and a cluster of private apartments on the floors above. By the end of the 17th century it had ceased to be a purely defensive fortress and, according to a description of 1693, was 'flanked on the south with very pretty gardens and orchards, adorned with excellent tarrases'. These 'tarrases' and 'two dainty spring wells' in the caves hollowed out of the rock are the two oldest surviving features at Culzean.

It was Sir Thomas's bachelor descendant and namesake who in 1762, after a two-and-a-half-year legal dispute, established his right to succeed as the 9th Earl of Cassillis. An 'improving laird', the 9th Earl had been busy enclosing the Culzean estate and in 1760 had added a new wing to the old castle which stretched to the edge of the cliff. Naturally enough, he preferred to remain at Culzean rather than move to the then principal seat of the Kennedys, Cassillis House.

His brother David, another bachelor who succeeded as 10th Earl of Cassillis in 1775, took a similar view and concentrated his energies on improving Culzean still further. The farm manager, John Bulley, greatly increased the profits of the estate and the new Earl decided to make a big splash by bringing in the most celebrated architect of the day, Robert Adam (who had previously designed a new parish kirk at Kirkoswald for his brother).

Between 1777 and 1792 the irrepressible Adam radically rebuilt Culzean Castle in four stages. First, he 'squared up' the old tower house into the great south front – overlooking the 'tarrases' – and added a three-storey wing on either side. Some of the masonry of the old tower was incorporated within the central block. Adam also built a new kitchen block at the east end of the 9th Earl's 1760 wing.

Next, in 1779, Adam added a round brewhouse, a milkhouse, bath-house and bedrooms to the west end of the 9th Earl's wing, and the wing itself was modified. However, not content with all this tinkering about, Adam – who according to the contemporary observer, John Clark, was encouraged by the 10th Earl of Cassillis 'without control…to indulge to the utmost his romantic and fruitful genius' – then proceeded to knock down the 9th Earl's wing in 1785.

In its place, between the kitchen block and the brewhouse, rose the mighty Drum Tower, with rooms on either side of it. The Saloon, the principal room in the Drum Tower, gave Adam the marvellous opportunity, brilliantly grasped, of contrasting the characteristics of 18th-century elegance with the wild scenery of sea, sky and mountain irresistibly framed in the windows. Immediately below the windows, 150 feet below, are the rocks with the breakers of the Firth of Clyde crashing into them; and, far across the water, lie the low line of the Mull of Kintyre, the Goatfell on Arran and, away to the north, the hills around the entrance to Loch Fyne. It is a thrill to stand in this circular interior and savour such a *coup de théâtre*.

PRECEDING PAGES The garden front of the castle and the viaduct framed by Robert Adam's 'ruined' arch.

LEFT The Dining Room, originally planned as two rooms – a library and a dressing room – but thrown into one during the 1870s alterations of Wardrop & Reid for the 3rd Marquess of Ailsa.

ABOVE The Armoury, mostly comprising weapons issued to the West Lowland Fencible Regiment when it was raised in the early 1800s by the 12th Earl of Cassillis (later 1st Marquess of Ailsa) to meet the threat of invasion by Napoleon. Even then the weapons tended to the antique.

Having taken Culzean Castle to the very edge of the cliff and gone a long way to unifying the building, Adam had, nonetheless, not finished yet. There was a space in the centre; he had forgotten to give the castle a grand staircase in the central well. What was to be done? In order to create enough room for his 1787 plans for the Oval Staircase he had to pull down the 'back half' of the tower-house. By a masterly stroke of genius he managed to transform what had been a gloomy space into the central interior of the castle. As David Learmont of the National Trust for Scotland has pointed out, Adam 'made it appear that the staircase, rather than being the last part to be built, was the first part, and the rest of the castle had been designed around it'.

LEFT A corner of Robert Adam's peerless circular Saloon. The Louis XVI chairs are covered in Beauvais tapestry; the carpet is actually a copy (made locally, at Irvine) of the one Adam designed for the room.

RIGHT The Oval Staircase: Adam's afterthought.

Detail of urn, with rams'- heads base.

The decoration of the interior carried on until 1795, three years after Adam died. The great architect had designed almost everything the eye could see – furniture and fittings, tables, mirrors, sconces and carpets. Outside, he had busied himself to build the stables enclosing the forecourt, the home farm on the next headland up the coast and the highly romantic mock ruined arch and causeway which now formed the principal approach to the castle.

Understandably all this activity – a 'most arduous undertaking' as it was described at the time – took its toll on the 10th Earl of Cassillis, a martyr to gout. 'I hope,' he wrote to his doubtless concerned banker in 1790, 'my operations will [soon] be at an end for I am really wearied of Building and wish to be at rest.' In the event, he died the same year as his architect, in 1792. Together they had achieved a masterpiece.

Culzean then acquired an American connection, which has remained strong to this day, when the Earldom of Cassillis passed to a kinsman Captain Archibald Kennedy, RN. He had retired from the Navy to No. 1 Broadway, New York, where his father had been Collector of Customs – though during the War of American Independence his house was requisitioned by none other than George Washington. The American Earl's son and successor, another Archibald, was a friend of the bluff 'Sailor King', William IV (one of whose illegitimate daughters, Lady Augusta FitzClarence, married the Earl's second son, John Kennedy-Erskine of the House of Dun – *qv*). The King created the Earl Marquess of Ailsa for his Coronation in 1831. Earlier in the 19th century, during the Napoleonic Wars, Culzean's strategic situation by the coast was exploited once more: gun emplacements were installed along the cliff top to the west of the house and the West Lowland Fencible Regiment were raised to defend Ayrshire against invasion. Their magnificent display of flintlock pistols and cavalrymen's swords now adorns the Entrance Hall.

For all its splendour, Culzean had been built for a Georgian bachelor and in Victorian times the 3rd Marquess of Ailsa found it too cramped for his large family. Messrs Wardrop & Reid were duly summoned to build the west wing, on the site of Adam's brewhouse, in 1879.

It was the 3rd Marquess's second son, the childless 5th Marquess of Ailsa, who, in 1945, offered Culzean and its glorious 560-acre 'policies' to the National Trust for Scotland. Looking back, one is struck by the Trust's supreme

The wild romanticism of the scenery outside Culzean contrasts thrillingly with the cool Classicism inside.

courage in taking it on. At the time many thought the gamble not so much courageous as foolhardy. Here, after half-a-dozen years of war and in an era of austerity when there was nothing like today's support for such ventures, was this tiny voluntary conservation agency (total membership 1,200; total free funds £5,000) accepting an unendowed historic property into inalienable care 'for the benefit of the nation'. The question was whether it would make or break the NTS.

It made the Trust. This extraordinary act of faith was to have immense significance in the history of the Heritage movement for at Culzean the NTS enterprisingly demonstrated the need for new legislation, agencies and

A shore silhouette of the castle and, on the distant horizon, the looming shadow of Ailsa Craig.

techniques which have borne wider fruit. In the 1950s Culzean was among the first beneficiaries of grants made by the Historic Buildings Council set up by the Historic Buildings and Ancient Monuments Act of 1953. In the 1960s Culzean became Scotland's first 'Country Park', complete with ranger service, young naturalists' club, a treetop walkway, deer park and visitors' centre in Adam's old home-farm buildings.

Many of the myriad buildings in the park had long been in need of repair and in 1990 the NTS launched a £5 million Culzean Appeal. Gradually these sandstone structures, weathered by the elements, are being restored. They range from Adam's great Viaduct to a beguiling series of follies and smaller build-ings (not all by Adam himself) such as the Gazebo, the Pagoda (or Monkey House), the Camellia House, the Dolphin House and the enchanting 'Cat Gates', so-called because of the seated Coade stone Egyptian lionesses on the piers.

The American links with Culzean have been a vital element in the National Trust for Scotland's fundraising. These were strengthened after the Second World War when the 5th Marquess of Ailsa asked that the Trust present General Eisenhower, Supreme Commander of the Allied Forces in Europe, with a flat in the top of the castle for his lifetime. 'I assured the Scottish Trust,' wrote 'Ike', 'that nothing else that Scotland could have done could so emphatically symbolize for me the feeling of British–American partnership which was such a vital force in bringing the war to a successful conclusion.' Although, unlike nine other American Presidents, the 34th President of the United States was not of Scots ancestry, his association with Culzean (christened the 'Scottish White House') surely made him into an honorary Caledonian. One suspects the attractions of the place for Ike were enhanced by the proximity of Turnberry and Troon golf courses – 'PRESIDENT ROUND IN 78', as a spoof headline in a Boulting Brothers film once screamed.

A special exhibition commemorating Ike, and his visits to Culzean, is one of the many attractions that have made Culzean such a deservedly popular showplace. It is a triumphant example of the precept laid down by the stalwarts of the NTS, Sir Jamie Stormonth Darling and Robin Prentice, in their publication *Culzean: The Continuing Challenge*: 'If the decision is right, the money will follow.'

21

GOSFORD HOUSE

ORE SEA, more Robert Adam. Yet at Gosford in East Lothian the maritime views seem not to have been as significant to the new house's patron, the 7th Earl of Wemyss, as the need to be closer to his beloved golf links; and Adam's original building has been much altered over the last two centuries – partly by other architectural hands and partly by a disastrous fire during the Second World War. Nonetheless, Gosford House, which remains the home of the present Earl of Wemyss, is an interesting example of Adam's later work (it was begun in 1790, only two years before his death), while William Young's late 19th-century Italianate south wing contains an astounding Marble Hall that must rank as one of Scotland's very grandest interiors.

Although today James Ramsay's Picturesque late 18th-century 'pleasure ground' at Gosford, linked by a series of ponds, is regarded as one of the best surviving examples, however overgrown, of this landscape style in Scotland, the Golfing Earl's choice of situation on the wasteland adjoining the Firth of Forth between Longniddry and Aberlady excited the scorn of his contemporaries. The precocious 5th Duke of Rutland, up here on a visit in 1796, found it 'objectionable in the highest degree: a barren rabbit warren on a sandy shore stretching on all sides and the country around being totally destitute of wood or fertilization'.

Nor did the architecture please all comers. In 1799 Lady Louisa Stuart, daughter-in-law of the Prime Minister Earl of Bute, observed: 'There is a *corps-de-logis* and two great pavilions, all with domes, so at a distance it looks like three great ovens but the front is really a very pretty one. They say the plan is absurd; three rooms in the middle of [a front] 50 feet long, each lined with one huge Venetian window and unconnected with the rest.'

In fairness to Robert Adam, it should be emphasized that after his death those windows were enlarged out of all proportion at the insistence of the Golfing Earl, who wanted as much light as possible to show off his collection of

Dutch and English pictures. Indeed the only unaltered part of Robert Adam's design at Gosford is the typically elegant stable block, some 300 yards to the east of the main house.

The house was completed in 1800 (the date on the pediment on the west facade), though in fact the Golfing Earl never took up residence because he is said to have found it too damp. Similarly, his grandson and successor, the 8th Earl of Wemyss, preferred to stay put at Amisfield nearby, or at Old Gosford House, a 17th-century building (which was to be enlarged by the architect William Burn in the 1830s).

The Amisfield estate had been inherited by the Golfing Earl from his maternal family of Charteris. His father, the 5th Earl of Wemyss, had eloped with Janet, only child and heiress of the rich rake Colonel Francis Charteris of Amisfield. 'No woman', according to a stern footnote in *The Complete Peerage*, 'was safe' from the notorious Colonel (featured in Hogarth's *Harlot's Progress*), who was once sentenced to death for rape, but escaped the block. 'A successful and unscrupulous gambler and money-lender', the Colonel acquired extensive estates which passed on his death in 1732 to his son-in-law on condition that he changed his name from Wemyss to Charteris.

Although he was the second son of the 5th Earl of Wemyss, the new Mr Charteris eventually succeeded – or he would have done had the title not been attainted owing to his exiled elder brother's support for Bonnie Prince Charlie – as *de jure* 7th Earl in 1786 and the ancestral Wemyss Castle estate in Fife passed to a younger brother, James. The Wemyss family had acquired

PRECEDING PAGES The magnificent Marble Hall in the Italianate south wing built by William Young for the 10th Earl of Wemyss in the 1880s.

BELOW Detail of lion on the steps of the east front.

BELOW The east (garden) front, with the south wing in the foreground.

RIGHT Corner of Marble Hall: Italian marble, Caen stone and alabaster.

BELOW Sphinx on the roof.

their eponymous lands on the coast opposite Gosford in medieval times. In the 13th century one of the family, Sir David de Wemyss, was among the lairds deputed to escort the child Queen Margaret, only surviving grandchild of King Alexander III, home from Norway. Unfortunately the young Queen died on the journey – with calamitous consequences for the Scots, if not for King Edward I of England.

The Wemysses rose to become Baronets and Earls in the 17th century. The 4th Earl, Lord High Admiral of Scotland to Queen Anne, was one of the commissioners for the Act of Union. Today Wemyss remains the seat of the cadet branch of the family and was until recently the home of Queen Victoria's last surviving godchild, Lady Victoria Wemyss, a remarkable centenarian celebrated for parking her motor-car on the steps of the castle in bizarre positions of which only a helicopter would be thought capable.

Meanwhile, back at Gosford, the 8th Earl of Wemyss toyed with the idea of radically altering his grandfather's house and consulted various architects, including the Classicist Sir Robert Smirke and possibly James Wyatt, then in his Gothic phase. In the event, he used none of their plans and contented himself

with pulling down Adam's flanking pavilions, or wings, leaving the centre block in solitary state for more than 50 years.

The 9th Earl of Wemyss – known as 'the Hunting Earl' and the dedicatee of *Mr Sponge's Sporting Tour* by R.S. Surtees – was in favour of pulling the place down altogether, but was dissuaded from this drastic action by his more aesthetically minded son and successor. John Ruskin, no less, described the 10th Earl of Wemyss as having 'a genuine devotion to art' and as 'an amateur artist of considerable skill'. In Ruskin's double-edged English view, 'There are not many men, and certainly not many Scotsmen, who possess the rare and undefinable gift of charm, which was undoubtedly his.'

This charm certainly comes across in the *Memories* of the 10th Earl. Of his wedding reception in Vienna, for example, he records that the hotel cook carved an ice in the shape of a rabbit – 'emblematic, perhaps, of a numerous progeny and of the family home, Gosford, founded on a rabbit warren'. He and his bride, Lady Anne Anson, daughter of the 1st Earl of Lichfield, duly produced a brood of nine and it was to house them, and his beloved pictures, in style that he commissioned the architect William Young to remodel Gosford.

The 10th Earl had a lifelong passion for collecting pictures, with a particular leaning towards the Italian Renaissance. He was blessed with a superb 'eye' – and a flair for spotting a bargain. His first purchase was a Carlo Dolci from a pawnbroker in London, and on his first visit to Italy in 1842 he acquired

LEFT The Gallery, top-lit to show off the great Dutch and Italian picture collections formed by the 7th and 10th Earls of Wemyss respectively.

BELOW LEFT View through the south courtyard.

two beautiful paintings from the proprietor of a café. Above all, Lord Wemyss was a genuine collector, who purchased pictures that he admired regardless of the vagaries of fashion, and did not employ agents – indeed he disapproved of any collector who 'bought through other men's eyes and paid through his own nose'.

To show off his masterpieces by Botticelli, Murillo, Rubens and the rest, Lord Wemyss chose an architect who had made his mark with his successful design for the War Office in London and had just won the competition for the new City Chambers in Glasgow. If William Young's external work on the two new wings may have perhaps been a little on the busy side, the interior of the surviving south wing is an overwhelming triumph.

The Marble Hall, a grand vision of pink alabaster, Caen stone and plasterwork, rises to a height of three storeys. A magnificent double staircase ascends to a surrounding gallery separated from the hall by a screen of Venetian windows reminiscent of Robert Adam's original design for the west front. The central dome, suspended by concealed cast-iron girders, is a work of great

RIGHT The Marble Hall: 'a photographer's dream'.

engineering skill by Sir William Arrol, and the whole concept owes much to the 'Art Earl', as he was nicknamed (though he was known as 'the Brigadier' in recognition of his founding the London Scottish Regiment). 'He has designed, I have planned,' noted Lord Wemyss in his memoirs about William Young (who was later to design another great marble hall, at Elveden in Suffolk for the 1st Earl of Iveagh).

And so in 1890 – seven years after succeeding to the Earldom and the estates but a century since building work had begun on the new house at Gosford – Lord Wemyss and his family finally moved in. Yet the great house's heyday was to be little more than a golden Edwardian afternoon. The Art Earl died, aged 95 (and with the proud record of having sat in Parliament for more than 70 years), in 1914 and subsequently Gosford was occupied only inter-mittently. The 11th Earl, who preferred to base himself at the ravishing Cotswold manor house of Stanway, ended up running Gosford as an hotel. On the outbreak of the Second World War it was requisitioned by the mili-tary; in 1940 one huge room in Adam's centre block was gutted by fire.

After the war extensive dry rot was discovered and in 1948 most of the roof of the north wing was taken off. Yet, three years later and to his eternal credit, the present Lord Wemyss and his family returned to live at Gosford, where he adapted the south wing, which had escaped the fire and (almost) the dry rot, into a self-contained house of its own. A keen conservationist, who was to be an outstanding Chairman and President of the National Trust for Scotland

ABOVE The present Earl of Wemyss winding one of his beloved clocks at Gosford.

BELOW Another view of the Gallery.

ABOVE A lion looks out across the Forth to Fife, ancestral county of the Wemysses.

BELOW A swan, atop an earl's coronet, surmounts the other heraldic beast of the family.

for many years, Lord Wemyss managed to re-roof the burnt-out part of the middle block with the help of grants from the Historic Buildings Council for Scotland in the 1980s.

The inside, though, partly under the new roof, remains stark and uninhabitable. After the opulence of the Marble Hall and the richness of its works of art, it comes as a shock to be confronted with the bare, plasterless stone walls of the burnt-out Saloon next door. Curiously enough, this dramatic interior space, with its irresistible air of ruinous romance, has a haunting quality all of its own.

The current plans for the future of Gosford include the restoration of the 1790 'pleasure ground' and – a project which would please the Golfing Earl – the construction of a new links golf course in the estate. Whatever happens to this great treasure-house, there is a bewitching element about Gosford, an air of lost romance waiting to be rediscovered.

22

ABBOTSFORD

ROXBURGHSHIRE

B Y THE narrow standards of an architectural purist, Abbotsford hardly qualifies as a 'great' house. John Ruskin was one of many to sneer at its architecture (a strange amalgam of 'Tudorbethan' and early 'Baronial'); even Queen Victoria herself found it 'rather gloomy'. Yet this extraordinarily atmospheric shrine to Sir Walter Scott has an enduring appeal which speaks out to the country-house visitor as no grander house ever does. So potent is Sir Walter's personality that you feel that he might, at any moment, pop his dome-like head round the door.

Sometimes one is even inclined to think that Scott actually invented Scotland. Certainly no one did more to re-invent Scottish traditions after the crushing of Scots pride at the Battle of Culloden, and to encourage the English 'discovery' of Scotland in the 19th century. His *Waverley* novels were charged with a romantic passion for an idealized Scottish past. What the late Colin McWilliam nicely described as 'the medievalistic gallimaufry of Abbotsford' is a delightful distillation of this cultural conjuring trick and is, of course, quite irresistible. To Scott himself it was an earthly paradise. 'I have seen much,' he used to say, 'but nothing like my ain house.'

A younger son of an Edinburgh solicitor, Walter, lamed for life as a toddler, was born in 1771 and spent his early years in the Borders, on his grandfather's farm, before being educated in the New Town. His love of the Border country never left him; the boy thrilled to stories about his ancestors such as Walter 'Beardie' Scott who was 'out' in the 1715 Jacobite Rising and vowed never to shave until the Stuarts were restored to the throne. As a young lawyer, serving as Sheriff-Depute of Selkirkshire, he would record all the local traditions and ballads he heard on his peregrinations.

When published, these ballads proved commercially successful and Scott went on to make a fortune with his own poems, such as *The Lay of the Last Minstrel*. With the royalties Scott was able to satisfy his modest ambition to become a Tweedside laird on a minor scale. In 1811, for £4,000, he bought a farmstead of some 110 acres (the estate was later to grow to 1,400 acres) called Cartleyhall on the south bank of the Tweed. Because the land had once belonged to Melrose Abbey, and there was a ford over the river by the house, Scott – with typical romanticism – decided to rename the property Abbotsford.

He slightly extended the rather basic farmhouse, where he installed his growing family, and turned to writing novels. They were phenomenally profitable. A vast new audience, hungry for romance about 'Olden Times', lapped up the *Waverley* novels in unprecedented quantities. Tales of Border life and Highland adventure (later supplemented by slices of medieval and Elizabethan pageantry) flowed from Scott's fluent pen. Suddenly the best-selling novelist found himself rich enough to expand his estate and enlarge his house.

A wing was added in 1818 and four years later Sir Walter (as he had become in 1820 upon his creation as a Baronet) was in a position to pull down the old farmhouse and build a new country house. William Atkinson, of Scone Palace fame (*qv*), was engaged as architect, with Edward Blore, an illustrator of books on Gothic whom Scott had discovered, contributing 'authentic' details.

With its battlemented tower, crow-stepped gables, conical turrets and strips of machicolation, all prefaced by castellated gateway and portcullis, Abbotsford could be described as being among the precursors of the style that was to become known as 'Scotch Baronial'. In many ways, it is undeniably absurd. As Mark Girouard has pointed out, from the outside it 'looks rather more like a toy house than a real one'. The big 19th-century windows filled with plate glass hardly harmonize with the old-style towers and gables.

Once inside, though, any Sassenach sniggers are swiftly swallowed. With its moulded ceilings and dark polished panelling and Sir Walter's magpie-style collections of curios, Abbotsford buzzes with vitality. This is no faked-up sham but the heartfelt expression of a warm and potent imagination.

PRECEDING PAGES *Sir Walter's 'Baronial' vision: the east elevation from the walled garden.*

BELOW *Patricia Maxwell-Scott (right) and her sister Dame Jean, plus canine friends, outside the conservatory.*

The entrance front.

ABOVE   A corner of the drawing room in the family wing.

RIGHT   The dining room in the family wing.

BELOW   The drawing room in the family wing.

ABOVE Corridor in the family wing.

LEFT Silhouette of Sir Walter at work.

RIGHT The writer's Study – as if the great man had just popped out for a moment.

The Entrance Hall, for instance, contains oak panelling from the Auld Kirk at Dunfermline, bloodthirsty arms and armour of every date, a model of Robert the Bruce's skull, a stone fireplace copied from the cloisters of Melrose Abbey, relics of the Battle of Waterloo, an elk's head, a riot of heraldry – and so mind-bogglingly on. Yet somehow it all hangs together, like an intensely personal mosaic.

Scott's powerful personality projects itself down the centuries and pervades the house. Among the mementoes on view are the last clothes he wore – a grey beaver hat, a black cutaway coat and plaid trousers. You feel his presence most strongly in the book-galleried study, with his small writing desk made of wood supposedly from the ships of the Spanish Armada.

In the Library, Scott, as portrayed in marble by Sir Francis Chantrey (the bust placed here in the niche previously occupied by Shakespeare on the day of Sir Walter's funeral in 1832), holds pride of place. One of the books that most influenced him, an early 18th-century *Life of Rob Roy* lies open in a showcase alongside such cherished objects as Rob Roy's purse and a lock of Bonnie Prince Charlie's hair. Among the cornucopia of other curios to be seen at Abbotsford are the Marquess of Montrose's sword and an engraved tumbler that belonged to Robert Burns ('the boast of Scotland', as Scott called him).

A measure of the respect and affection which Sir Walter Scott inspired is shown by the presents on display: a medallion portrait of Goethe (passed on by the hand of Thomas Carlyle); a silver urn from Lord Byron; and an ebony desk and set of chairs from King George IV which adorns the Drawing Room, hung with Chinese 18th-century painted paper. On meeting the novelist during his highly emotional royal visit to Scotland in 1822, the King (attired in flesh-coloured tights under his kilt) exclaimed: 'Sir Walter Scott! The man in Scotland I most wish to see!'

The King's visit, which Scott himself largely stage-managed, was perhaps the zenith of the novelist's career. Four years later came the nadir. The printing firm of Ballantyne, in which he was a sleeping partner, collapsed with spectacular debts, brought about by an unwise involvement with a London publisher.

ABOVE Bonnie Prince Charlie.

LEFT Corner full of curios.

Sir Walter's 'Baronial' hall, awash with armour.

Scott, at the age of 55 and having only completed the rebuilding of his beloved Abbotsford a couple of years before, found himself faced with liabilities of £116,000 (several millions in today's money).

He could have avoided them by going bankrupt, but he was far too honourable a man to escape what he saw as his responsibility. Instead, he buckled down to grinding out the millions of words that were to pay off all the debts – and, doubtless, to destroy his health. One lingers in his Study, scene of so much unremitting toil, with sympathy and doubly renewed respect.

Yet the mood at Abbotsford is far from gloomy for Scott was a warm, lovable man, never happier than when working alongside his foresters in the woods or walking his devoted dogs. Canine characters enliven the picture collection at Abbotsford, whether Percy the greyhound as depicted by Sir Henry Raeburn or Ginger the terrier by Sir Edwin Landseer.

Sir Walter's famous last words to his son-in-law and biographer, J.G. Lockhart, are one of the most attractive aspects of the Scott tradition. 'My dear,' he said, 'be a good man. Be virtuous, be religious, be a good man. Nothing else will give you any comfort when you come to lie here.' As the Laird lay dying in what is now the Dining Room at Abbotsford, Lockhart observed: 'It was so quiet a day that the sound he best loved, the gentle ripple of the Tweed over its pebbles, was distinctly audible as we knelt around his bed.'

Abbotsford had already become a place of pilgrimage before Sir Walter's death in 1832 and now it was opened regularly to the public. The volume of visitors proved so strong that in the 1850s J.R. Hope-Scott, QC, who married the eventual heiress of Abbotsford, Charlotte Lockhart (J.G.'s daughter), built a new family wing on to one side of the house.

This wing, which contains a simple chapel, remains the home of Sir Walter's present-day descendants and the châtelaines of Abbotsford, Patricia Maxwell-Scott and her sister Dame Jean, daughters of the late Major-General Sir Walter Maxwell-Scott, 1st and last Bt (Charlotte Lockhart's grandson), who won the DSO and was mentioned in despatches six times during the First World War. With their friendly, unaffected manner, keen sense of history and delightful dogs, the two Scott sisters uphold Abbotsford's hospitable traditions.

Any doubts as to the inclusion of Abbotsford among Scotland's great houses were dispelled by the reaction of the present writer's son, and long-suffering driver, to the *genius loci*. A glut of palatial seats in the Borders had left him 'housed-out', but the charms of Abbotsford ignited a genuine spark of enthusiasm. Sir Walter's spirit lives on.

ABOVE Liveried firebuckets.

RIGHT The conservatory framed in the arch leading to the walled garden.

BELOW A stone dog guards the private entrance to the family wing.

23

BOWHILL

SELKIRK

'HEN summer smiled on sweet Bowhill,' sang Sir Walter Scott in *The Lay of the Last Minstrel*, 'And July's eve, with balmy breath,/Watch the blue-bells on Newark Heath...' The Laird of Abbotsford (*qv*), who was touchingly proud of his kinship with the great Border dynasty of Scott of Buccleuch, plays a significant role in the story of Bowhill. He had the aged Last Minstrel recite his Lay at Newark Castle, one of the Scott strongholds (now a ruin) a couple of miles up the River Yarrow from the present Bowhill House, which is full of associations with the Border balladeer.

A close friend and mentor of the 4th Duke of Buccleuch, who shared his romantic passion for Border life, Sir Walter dedicated *The Lay of the Last Minstrel* to his wife ('my lovely chieftainess', as Scott described her). The manuscript of *The Lay* is now to be found in the Study at Bowhill, alongside the author's plaid and other relics. The room is dominated by Sir Henry Raeburn's celebrated portrait of Sir Walter (a different version of the one at Abbotsford – *qv*), this time with his faithful dog Camp at his feet.

As at the Buccleuchs' other seat of Drumlanrig (*qv*), Sir Walter also took a close interest in the building improvements at Bowhill. Both the 4th and 5th Dukes benefited from his advice as the plain box-like early 18th-century house was transformed in the 19th century into first a Classical villa (to the designs of William Atkinson, also the architect of Abbotsford) and then into a Victorian pile (under the supervision of William Burn, who at the outset urged Sir Walter 'to promote my interest with the [5th] Duke').

The early 18th-century 'box' had been built by the Murray family, who had acquired the property from the Scotts in the 1690s. This, though, was merely an interregnum as Bowhill was in traditional Scott territory, and in 1745 the 2nd Duke of Buccleuch bought it back as an estate for his younger son. The 2nd Duke's marriage to the Queensberry heiress of Drumlanrig (*qv*) in 1720 had united the two families historically associated with the estate, for the ancient

PRECEDING PAGES The south front reflected in the water.

LEFT The Upper Gallery of the Gallery Hall, or 'Sallon', with its set of Mortlake tapestries (1670) of *The Triumph of Julius Caesar* based on Andrea Mantegna's cartoons at Hampton Court.

ABOVE Detail of Meissen vase in Drawing Room.

BELOW Lower Gallery of the Gallery Hall: 18th-century French furniture and 17th-century portraits.

Ettrick Forest, embracing the present Bowhill estate, was granted by Robert the Bruce to the Douglases in the 14th century. Subsequently it reverted to the Crown and was a favourite hunting ground for the Kings of Scotland who used Newark Castle as a hunting box. Various Scotts were active as Rangers of the forest from the 12th century. The legend has it that one day, deep in a 'cleuch', or ravine, in the Rankil Burn, a young Scott seized a cornered buck by the antlers and threw it over his shoulder to save the King's life – hence the origin of the name Buccleuch ('Buck-Cleuch').

In any event, the forest was distributed mainly to members of the Scott family in about 1550 and the first one to establish himself in a big way was Sir Walter Scott (known as 'Bold Buccleuch' for his daring rescue of 'Kinmount Willie' from Carlisle Castle in 1596), who was created the 1st Lord Scott of Buccleuch. Bold Buccleuch's son was advanced to an Earldom and later in the 17th century the Scott heiress, Anne, who married the ill-fated Duke of Monmouth (natural son of King Charles II and Lucy Walters), was created Duchess of Buccleuch in her own right.

As things turned out, Bowhill's future role as a subsidiary family seat was short-lived and it found itself promoted to higher billing. Lord Charles Scott, the second surviving son of the 2nd Duke of Buccleuch, for whom the property was intended, only survived a couple of years after its purchase and, following

The Drawing Room, created in 1831 when two rooms, one of them the original front hall on the south, were thrown together. The crimson wallcoverings, faded to pale pink in places, date from the room's conversion. To the right is Sir Joshua Reynolds's celebrated portrait of the Montagu heiress, Elizabeth, who married the 3rd Duke of Buccleuch, together with her daughter, Lady Mary Scott.

the deaths of his elder brother and their father shortly afterwards, Bowhill passed to Lord Charles's young nephew, the 3rd Duke of Buccleuch. The 3rd Duke – who united the Scotts with the great house of Montagu of Boughton by his marriage in 1767 to Lady Elizabeth Montagu, eventual heiress of the Duke of Montagu – carried out some planting on the Bowhill estate. A one-time pupil of the economist Adam Smith, author of *The Wealth of Nations*, the 3rd Duke was an enlightened and progressive landowner with a dedication to dynamic and efficient land management that has remained the hallmark of the Bowhill estate to this day.

The 3rd Duke does not seem to have lived in the old house at Bowhill – hardly surprising, in view of his myriad palaces elsewhere – but his son, the future 4th Duke, began using it as an occasional summer house in the early years of the 19th century. Then, on succeeding to the Dukedom in 1812, he commissioned William Atkinson to add what amounted to a complete new Classical villa (including a central Saloon) to the south side of the existing house.

The remodelling appears to have been completed by 1814, though it was soon apparent that the new house was not big enough. Atkinson was duly asked to design flanking wings. First came the east wing, containing the Dining Room, and then, in 1819, the west. 'My prodigious undertaking of building a west wing to be added to the body of Bowhill is already begun,' the 4th Duke wrote in what was to be his last letter to Sir Walter Scott (February 15, 1819):

A library is to be added to the present drawing room... I think this addition will add much to our comforts and convenience. It gives me a bedroom, dressing room (which I shall use as a depository for guns and

The Dining Room, added to the east of the house by William Atkinson in 1814/15 for the 4th Duke of Buccleuch ('the Pink Boy' by Sir Joshua Reynolds to the right of the fireplace). To the left is Reynolds's exceptionally charming portrait of Lady Caroline Scott, muffled up as 'Winter'. On the far wall, to the right, is Canaletto's masterly study of Whitehall.

LEFT Detail of caryatid supporting marble chimney-piece in Dining Room.

BELOW Detail of silver candelabrum by Robert Garrard of London (1830, weighing 13 stone, at a cost of £3,641) in the Dining Room. It depicts the traditional origin of the title Buccleuch – when a bold Scott saved the King's life by manhandling a cornered buck in a cleuch.

fishing tackle), a sitting room and a servants room, all connecting. The sitting room connects with the library by a sham book door.

Alas, the 4th Duke did not live long to enjoy such 'comforts and convenience', dying a few months later. His son Walter Francis, the 5th Duke, brought in William Burn from 1831 onwards to enlarge Bowhill. The main entrance was moved round to the north side, thereby making the south front private, and within the house the staircase was moved to the west, the Saloon was enlarged by taking in the cross corridor and the Drawing Room was extended by taking in Atkinson's entrance hall and porch.

Burn was to work off and on at Bowhill for nearly 40 years. Even after his death in 1870 the work was carried on by his nephew J. MacVicar Anderson, who was responsible for the Chapel, Billiard Room and Smoking Room. The result is that Bowhill grew and grew into a vast rambling house; joined, as it is, to the stables, the whole frontage forms a continuous unit of 437 feet.

Yet, for all the improving Victorian zeal of the 5th Duke and his architects, they never lost sight of the fact that Bowhill is essentially a Georgian house. As John Cornforth has pointed out, Burn 'had to accept the extreme restraint of Atkinson's classicism' – on the outside, at least; within he was able to be more eclectic in the decoration.

No one could argue much of a case for Bowhill's architectural merits. On a grey day the exterior can look distinctly austere. However, its glorious setting (enhanced in the 19th century by the talents of the landscape designer and watercolourist William Sawrey Gilpin), remarkably homely atmosphere (notwithstanding its size) and, above all, its fabulous collections of treasures combine to give Bowhill a special place among the great houses of Scotland.

The sheer quality of the contents impress one the moment a visitor enters the towering Sallon, or Gallery Hall as it is now more familiarly known. Up above Burn's balustrade, the eye takes in three Mortlake tapestries (woven after Mantegna's cartoons of *The Triumph of Julius Caesar* at Hampton Court). Below hang splendid portraits by Sir Peter Lely and Sir Anthony Van Dyck. Here, too, is a sumptuous feast of French furniture, a Boulle bracket clock, pale blue Sèvres bowls mounted in ormolu – and an exquisite Louis XIV mirror of ebony, tortoiseshell and ormolu, given by King Charles II to his son, the Duke of Monmouth.

ABOVE 'General Monk's bed' from a room at Dalkeith Palace which Monk used when planning the Restoration of the monarchy after Cromwell.

RIGHT The Library, which is the principal living room of the present Duke and Duchess of Buccleuch when they are in residence and which is not part of the public tour. It has been little changed since 1814, save for the installation of the white marble chimneypiece from Dalkeith in 1948. The 'A' monogram indicates that it was made (in 1705) for the Scott heiress, the Duke of Monmouth's widow, Anne Duchess of Buccleuch – whose portrait by William Wissing surmounts the overmantel.

The Monmouth Room (built as a chapel in the 1870s) is dedicated to the Duke's memory and contains such relics as his magnificent saddle (worked in gold thread) and the white linen shirt in which he was executed in 1685 after the crushing of his Rebellion. As well as portraits of the Duke (by Lely) and Duchess (by Sir Godfrey Kneller), the Monmouth Room pictures include a series of topographical views by the 18th-century landscapist George Barret.

The finest topographical work at Bowhill, though, is, of course, Canaletto's luminous view of Whitehall, which hangs harmoniously with a dazzling display of family portraits (notably by Sir Joshua Reynolds and Thomas Gainsborough) in the Dining Room. Reynolds's charming study of the muffled Lady Caroline Scott (sister of the 4th Duke) as *Winter* would come high on many people's list of their favourite pictures.

In the Drawing Room (with its faded silk brocade and curtains of the 1840s) there is yet another fine Reynolds, of the Montagu heiress who became the wife of the 3rd Duke. Here the pictures, including a couple of Claude Lorraines and one of Jacob van Ruysdael's greatest landscapes, almost take second place to the superb sets of French furniture.

It is tempting to drool on about the marvellous treasures of Bowhill, which have been greatly enhanced this century since the closure of two of the Buccleuchs' other palaces, Montagu House in London and Dalkeith, near Edinburgh (now let to an American university). Yet, as the present Duke of

LEFT A Buccleuch bicycle: Bowhill remains very much a family home.

BELOW Terrace view on south front.

The south front stretching towards the stables.

Buccleuch points out, Bowhill is 'much more than a great family home, with a unique art collection in the setting with which it is historically associated'. It is, he stresses, the focal point of the estate.

Successive Dukes of Buccleuch have traditionally regarded the care and productivity of the land, together with the well-being of everyone upon it, as a primary duty. The 5th Duke, Walter Francis, whose tenure at Bowhill stretched for 65 years, spoke these lapidary words when opening a fête in 1839:

> What has been entrusted to me has not been given that it might be wasted in idle or frivolous amusements; nor would I be justified in wasting the hard earnings of the tillers of the soil by carrying them away and spending them in foreign countries, but I wish to see them employed as the means of producing good to them and to the country at large.

The present Duke, like his father before him, echoes this view and has dedicated his considerable energies to 'demonstrating that it is on a private agricultural estate, such as this, that the conflict of interests between farming, forestry, conservation, amenity and sport can most successfully be reconciled to the local and national advantage'. Besides opening the house every July, the Duke also regularly opens part of the estate as a 'Country Park', complete with prize-winning educational facilities, adventure playground and nature trails along the lochs and rivers of this Border paradise.

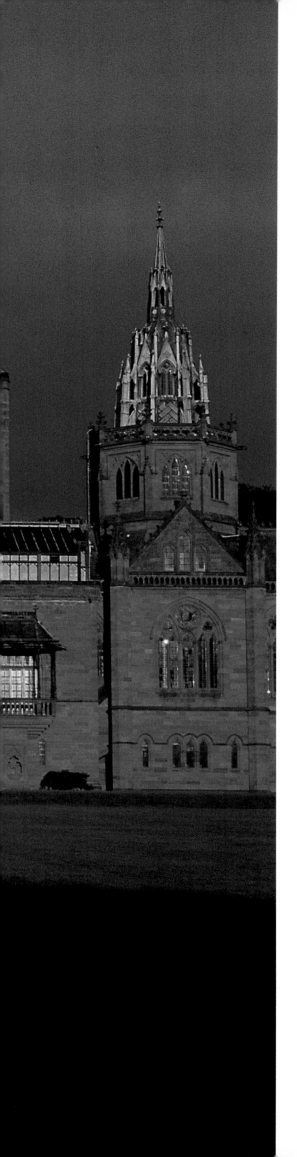

24

MOUNT STUART

VISIT to Mount Stuart on the still pleasingly unspoilt Isle of Bute tends to leave one deprived of the power of speech. Like an old hippy, one finds oneself mouthing such inanities as, 'That's something else, man, far out...' Such New Age argot may perhaps, be explained by the dazzling array of astrological mumbo-jumbo incorporated into the design of this amazing Gothic extravaganza built for the 3rd Marquess of Bute, one of the richest and certainly one of the most unusual aristocrats of the late 19th century.

The mystical Marquess was born – as we can tell from the elaborate astrological ceiling of his bedroom, which depicts the position of the planets at the time of his nativity – on September 12, 1847, at Mount Stuart, then a rather barrack-like Georgian box (originally designed by Alexander McGill in 1716 and remodelled by George Paterson in 1780). His father, the 2nd Marquess of Bute, who had secured the family fortune by transforming Cardiff, on his Welsh estates, into a major port, died only six months later. The infant Marquess was to enjoy a great inheritance.

His father descended from the Royal House of Stuart, a line long seated at Rothesay Castle on the Isle of Bute, of which the head of the family was Hereditary Keeper. The 2nd Marquess also inherited the Earldom of Dumfries from his maternal grandfather and accordingly prefixed his surname with Crichton.

The most prominent member of the family had been the 3rd Earl of Bute, King George III's much-maligned Prime Minister. For all the bad press he has received from historians – William Lecky asserted that this royal favourite was 'disliked and distrusted by all with whom he had to deal' – this Lord Bute was an admirable patron of literature and the fine arts, as well as an ardent botanist. Many of the non-Victorian contents at Mount Stuart today came from the Prime Minister Bute's splendid collections of paintings (notably of the 17th century) and furniture formerly housed at his Bedfordshire seat of Luton Hoo, which was rebuilt for him by his fellow Scot, Robert Adam.

PRECEDING PAGES The early morning light hits the windows of the east (garden) front.

LEFT View up to the stained glass above the third-floor gallery of the Marble Hall.

RIGHT The vaulted Marble Staircase. The decorative paintings in the spandrels of the arches (illustrating the Days of Creation) and the heraldic glass in the windows were executed by H.W. Lonsdale.

BELOW Another view of the Marbled Staircase.

The 3rd Marquess's own passion for art and architecture knew no bounds. Not for nothing is the ceiling of the Horoscope Room at Mount Stuart adorned with a frieze of miniature castles. Altogether he is reckoned to have sponsored some 60 building projects and to have acted as patron to a dozen architects, most famously the eccentric genius 'Billy' Burges, with whom he rebuilt much of Cardiff Castle. Its exotic interior became aglow with wall paintings and emblazoned heraldry. In Scotland the 3rd Marquess's myriad restoration schemes ranged from Falkland Palace to Dunblane Cathedral.

On coming of age in 1868 the 3rd Marquess caused a sensation by being received into the Roman Catholic Church. As an Oxford undergraduate on a tour of Palestine he had come 'to see very clearly that the Reformation in England and Scotland was the work neither of God nor the people, its real authors being wasteful and tyrannical kings and in Scotland a pack of greedy, time-serving and unpatriotic noblemen'. Benjamin Disraeli was inspired by Lord Bute's conversion to write his novel *Lothair*. The Marquess took to wearing a cloak like a monk's habit, studied Hebrew in order to translate the Roman Breviary and steeped himself in astrology, the occult and the lives of little-known Scottish saints. 'Isn't it perfectly monstrous,' he once exclaimed out of the blue to a bemused lady in a London drawing room, 'that St Magnus hasn't got an octave?'

Initially, Lord Bute's improvements at Mount Stuart on coming into his heritage were on a minor scale. Burges designed a new chapel for the old house,

which also acquired a new entrance hall, and the animal-loving Marquess introduced beavers and wallabies into the woods. Then, in 1877, the central block of the 18th-century house was gutted by fire.

This was the opportunity that Lord Bute had been waiting for. He commissioned the Edinburgh-born medievalist Robert Rowand Anderson (later Sir Robert and best known for his Scottish National Portrait Gallery), who had studied under the great Goth, Sir Gilbert Scott, in London. 'Anderson's plans are exceedingly nice,' wrote Lord Bute to his wife, the former Gwendolen Fitzalan-Howard (eldest daughter of the 1st Lord Howard of Glossop), in the autumn of 1879. 'The house seems to bid fair to be a splendid palace.'

No expense was to be spared. 'I have not made up my mind,' remarked Lord Bute to his friend Sir Herbert Maxwell as they studied a model of the new Mount Stuart complete with a great central hall to be surrounded by pillars, 'whether these pillars shall be marble or granite.' 'I suppose,' replied Sir Herbert, 'that granite would cost a good deal more than marble, being harder to work.' 'True,' said Lord Bute. 'I am told granite will cost £20,000 more than marble; but that's not the point. The question is which will look best.'

In the event, marbles were chosen, 'the rarest', as Lord Bute's friend and biographer, Abbot Sir David Hunter Blair, 5th Bt, a Benedictine monk, put it: '*pavonozetto*, emperor's red, *cipollino* columns crowned with capitals of purest white and arches of grey Sicilian'. The Marble Hall, to which they give their name, is reminiscent of a stupendous cathedral, lit by rich stained-glass (designed by H.W. Lonsdale) which projects bursts of colour on to the stonework. The sky-like ceiling, decorated by Charles Campbell, who worked with Burges at Cardiff, is a kaleidoscope of glinting, glass stars. Superlatives are inadequate for this astonishing interior.

By contrast with the exotic splendour of the Marble Hall, the Chapel is a vision of white purity, relieved only by the blood-red rays pouring in from the crimson stained glass. Michael Hall of *Country Life* has suggested that this most thrilling architectural effect of Mount Stuart – the transition from the dark, dappled richness of the Marble Hall to the blinding white Chapel – may have been in part inspired by the transformation scenes in Wagner's *Parsifal* 'in which the glades of Monsalvat dissolve into the chapel of the Holy Grail'.

ABOVE Madonna and the infant Jesus on external wall.

LEFT 'Was there ever such a hall for hide-and-seek?' asked the 3rd Marquess of Bute's friend and biographer, Abbot Sir David Hunter Blair, 5th Bt. Less prosaically he described this astonishing interior as a 'vast hall gleaming with light'.

RIGHT The Marble Hall arcade and *The Lord of the Hunt* tapestry, designed by William Skeoch Cumming – the first to be woven at the Dovecot Studio, established in Edinburgh by the 4th Marquess of Bute.

ABOVE The elaborate heraldic ceiling – a literal family tree – in the Drawing Room.

ABOVE The astrological ceiling of the Horoscope Room, showing the position of the planets at the time of the 3rd Marquess of Bute's birth on September 12, 1847.

RIGHT The Horoscope Room, the bedroom of the 3rd Marquess of Bute, leading to his observatory (now a conservatory).

Mount Stuart is so extraordinary that it has that sort of effect on sober architectural historians. Marcus Binney saw an echo of Philip II of Spain and the Escorial in Lord Bute's island fortress; the exterior of the four-square, massive Gothic pile also struck him as 'sheer and massive as the Doge's Palace in Venice'. To Gavin Stamp, Mount Stuart 'reflects the character of its creator: it is romantic and mysterious, deeply learned and eclectic, incorporating elements from several Continental as well as British sources into a unified whole'.

For the whole to become complete, though, took rather too long even for Lord Bute's delight in detail ('But why should I hurry over what is my chief pleasure?' he once protested). Anderson was eventually replaced, at the fitting-out stage of the interior, by Burges's assistant, William Frame, whose fondness for the bottle hardly hastened progress. 'Frame being drunk again,' noted Lord Bute in his diary in 1890, 'had to dismiss him.' Anderson was reinstated and building work resumed at a snail's pace. The Chapel (its lantern inspired by the one at Saragossa in Spain) was only begun in 1896, the eaves gallery around the west front in 1899.

Operations came to an abrupt halt the next year when Lord Bute died of a stroke, aged 53 (his heart being buried on the Mount of Olives). His widow, though, later proceeded with the finishing-off of such interiors as the Libraries and the swimming pool – a bizarre exercise in subterranean Gothic that puts one in mind of the secret lair of *The Phantom of the Opera*.

With the dawn of a new century there was a violent reaction against the perceived 'hideousness' of Victorian Gothic and in 1920 the 4th Marquess of Bute, otherwise a Classical conservationist and the first chairman of the Scottish National Buildings Record, went so far as to offer Mount Stuart for sale 'conditional to its complete demolition and removal by the Purchaser ... Suitable for re-erection as an Hotel, Hydro, Restaurant, Casino, Public Building, Etc.'

Fortunately for posterity there were no takers. Sixty years on, the 6th Marquess of Bute, an inspirational chairman of both the National Trust for Scotland and the Historic Buildings Council for Scotland, nobly embarked, together with his second wife, Jennifer, and the conservation architect Stewart Tod, on a full-scale repair of the fabric and restoration of the interiors. The 3rd Marquess's ambitious project had never been fully completed and now his far-sighted great-grandson assembled a talented team of young artists and crafts people to finish the job.

The Marble Hall was cleaned, its glass stars refitted, the stained-glass windows releaded, the mullions regilded. The Chapel was also cleaned, its upper steeple being decoratively painted. The Dining Room was rehung with a Crace wallpaper; the overmantel by John Adam in the Red Drawing Room triumphantly restored. The 3rd Marquess's observatory became a conservatory; the Horoscope Room, as we have seen, brilliantly recreated. Outside, the roof was completely overhauled, the stonework repointed. A new 'family entrance', with carvings by Dick Reid, was also created on the west side of the house. As in all worthwhile restorations – and this was a magnificent one – Lord and Lady Bute added an extra dimension of their own ideas to the project.

The renovation, indeed rejuvenation, of Mount Stuart was a vital part of Lord Bute's scheme to vest the house itself, the policies (also given a major overhaul) and entire estate in a charitable trust. Its principal objective was 'to preserve Mount Stuart House, policies and estate as an integral unit'. Lord Bute saw this dream become a reality before his tragically early death in 1993.

Today the Mount Stuart Trust opens the house and gardens 'as a centre for the wider enjoyment and better understanding of their unique historical, architectural, cultural and botanical features'. What the late Marquess's elder son and heir, the former racing driver Johnny Dumfries (joint winner of Le Mans in 1988), nicely described in a tribute to his father as Mount Stuart's 'outrageous beauty' has been stylishly preserved for future generations. And Johnny Dumfries is carrying on his father's good work with infectious enthusiasm.

LEFT The Drawing Room, divided by screens of marble columns. The ceiling was coloured in 1899.

BELOW Looking out across the roofscape to the Firth of Clyde and the Ayrshire hills.

25

MANDERSTON

T MANDERSTON in the Borders we arrive – with a flamboyant
'Poop! Poop!' in the manner of Mr Toad – in the Edwardian era
when country-house comfort and opulence had attained its
apogee. This amazing custom-built dream world of sybaritic luxury
has rightly been called the swansong of the great Classical house.
Although some purists may find the exterior a touch ponderous
and ungainly, notwithstanding the razor-sharp masonry, the 'Adam
Revival' interiors are of a breathtaking quality. The attention to detail throughout the house and its policies is absolutely tip-top; the materials and craftsmanship
are of a standard that can only be described as unique – in the case of the
Silver Staircase literally so, for it is the only one of its kind in the world.

This enviable Edwardian paradise was created for Sir James Miller, 2nd Bt,
a famous figure on the Turf known as 'Lucky Jim', by the architect John Kinross.
Lucky Jim's father, Williiam, who had made a fortune trading hemp and herring
with the Russians, bought the estate in 1860 on the death of his brother Richard,
who had acquired it five years earlier. The property then consisted of a square
late-Georgian box, originally built for a Mr Dalhousie Weatherstone in the 1790s,
probably to the designs of Alexander Gilkie or John White.

William Miller, who was a Liberal MP rumoured never to have spoken in the
House of Commons, aggrandized – or to be less polite, mucked about with –
the old house in 1871 to the designs of an architect called John Simpson. A
pillared entrance porch was added and extra servants' bedrooms installed under
a bizarre new Frenchified roof.

Three years later William Miller was created a Baronet on the recommen-
dation of William Gladstone, grateful for Miller's well-contrived political dinners.
In the same year, 1874, his eldest son and namesake fatally choked on a cherry
stone at Eton and so Manderston passed to the second son, Lucky Jim.

As *Vanity Fair* magazine pointed out in 1890, the new Baronet, 'being a
good fellow, one of the most wealthy commoners in the country and a bachelor,

he is a very eligible young man'. In the event, he married Eveline Curzon, daughter of the 4th Lord Scarsdale and younger sister of the great George Nathaniel Curzon, soon to be appointed Viceroy of India. The splendid Curzon family seat of Kedleston in Derbyshire, Robert Adam's masterpiece, obviously made a strong impression on Sir James Miller; Manderston resounds with echoes of its delicate palatial grandeur. Here, surely, was a case of Lucky Jim showing his by then somewhat impoverished in-laws (the 4th Lord Scarsdale was a clergyman) that anything they could do he could do better.

Before his marriage in 1893 Sir James had already begun improving Manderston. New garden terraces and a horse-shoe stair was added to the south front by Kinross in 1890. For his bride he commissioned the same architect to build a boathouse in the form of an Alpine chalet.

In the spirit of the age, sport took a high priority for Lucky Jim, who was an excellent shot as well as a racehorse owner. In 1895 Kinross built a game-keeper's cottage, kennels and a home farm on the estate, plus a stable block in the Classical manner which *Horse and Hound* magazine – not an authority to chuck gushing superlatives around – has recently remarked 'probably boasts the finest stabling in all the world'.

Where else, indeed, would you find barrel-vaulted roofs of selected teak above teak stalls with polished brass posts, tiled troughs (reminiscent of grand hotel basins) and such sumptuous equestrian accommodation? The names of the

PRECEDING PAGES *View of garden front and terraces.*

RIGHT *The only Silver Staircase in the world. In Manderston's Edwardian heyday it would take three men three weeks to dismantle, polish and put it back together. It was restored to its former glory in 1980.*

BELOW *The Hall: shades of Kedleston, the home of Sir James Miller's Curzon in-laws.*

fortunate animals which once occupied these luxurious chambers (all with the initial letter 'M', for Miller and Manderston) are incised on marble panels. The harness room is a leathery haven of rich rosewood, marble and brass.

If one thinks the horses were pampered at Manderston, the cows visiting the Marble Dairy around a delightful cloister must have assumed sacred status. Inside the milkhouse, the boss in the centre of the rib-vaulted roof featured a milkmaid at work. Manderston's own boss, though, Sir James Miller, spotted that the girl was sitting on the wrong side of the cow; the half-ton stone ornament had to be taken down and recarved.

Perfectionism was the order of the day; cost did not count. When John Kinross enquired as to how much he could spend on the complete remodelling of the main house, upon which Sir James Miller decided to embark when he returned from the Boer War in 1901, his patron airily replied: 'It simply doesn't matter.' Lucky Jim, lucky architect.

Kinross created a new north front with an imposing Ionic portico. Above the new main entrance door the Miller coat of arms bears the family motto, *Omne Bonum Supeme* ('All good comes from above'), a slight contradiction in terms as the family fortune derived from below, in the shape of herrings. Fulfilling his brief to provide plenty of accommodation for guests and servants, Kinross added a comfortable new bachelors' wing and converted the old stable block to the west of the house into an immaculate set of service rooms, including the laundry.

If the outside of the new house was a little austere (though the Peebles sandstone is enriched with carved medallions), in keeping with Classical restraint, the inside is an exuberant 'Adam' fantasy awash with apses, domes, covings and columns. It is fun to spot the allusions to Kedleston – such as the chimneypiece in the spacious central Hall (under its elaborately arabesqued dome); the ceiling in the Ballroom, cribbed from the dining room at Kedleston; and the display of Derbyshire Bluejohn in the house's own Dining Room.

LEFT The ceiling of the Drawing Room, incorporating the same colour scheme used by Robert Adam for the Library ceiling at the neighbouring Mellerstain (*qv*).

ABOVE The Drawing Room, opening into the
Ballroom, where Sir James and Lady Miller
threw their first and only ball, to celebrate
Manderston's completion in November 1905.

ABOVE Fanlight adorning the Hall.

LEFT View through the Hall, with organ in ante-room at foot of stairs.

RIGHT Corner of the Dining Room, with display of Derbyshire Bluejohn, a rare semi-precious stone mined only in that county – the ancestral territory of Lady Miller, née Curzon of Kedleston.

The Ballroom, which opens dramatically from the Drawing Room, conjures up a delicious floating sensation. It is decorated in Lucky Jim's racing colours of primrose and white which were best known for carrying his owner-bred horse Rock Sand to the Turf's 'Triple Crown' (the Two Thousand Guineas, Derby and St Leger) in 1903. Sir James lived up to his nickname: in 1890 he bought the horse Sanfoin only two days before the Derby and saw it romp home down the course at Epsom at odds of 25 to 1. Unlike many rich men, though, he relished his good fortune and he was a deservedly popular sportsman; the jockey Danny Meyer, in a letter displayed in the old servants' hall at Manderston, described Sir James as 'the *best* Master I've ever had'. Lucky Jim's Turf winnings of £118,000 over 16 years would have gone at least some way towards defraying his lavish expenditure at Manderston.

The gorgeous Louis XVI-style furniture, *le dernier cri* in sumptuous upholstery, was supplied by the fashionable firm of London decorators Charles Meiller & Co, who had already furnished the Millers' town house in Grosvenor Square. The elaborate wallhangings, curtains and other decorative adornments were mainly fitted up by the Edinburgh firm of Scott Morton & Co, with the weaving being carried out by Warners.

Vaulted Marble Dairy.

Done up as it was in the era of the *Entente Cordiale*, the French influence is strong at Manderston. The Silver Staircase (brilliantly restored in 1980 after not being cleaned for nearly 70 years) was inspired by the Petit Trianon. Even in the Marble Dairy one is reminded of Marie Antoinette, though the panelled room where Lady Miller took tea above is housed in a tower built to look like a Border Keep that could hardly be more Scottish.

In the handsomely stuccoed Dining Room, the last interior to be completed when the house was finished in 1905 and the only room on the ground floor to have been redecorated since Manderston was built, one's thoughts turn from the ceiling carved in high relief to fantasies about Edwardian breakfasts. That the pleasures of the table were well organized in this establishment is nicely illustrated by the six separate white-tiled larders downstairs: one each for ice, pastry, raw meat, cooked meat, game and fish (complete with fountain) – an arrangement to satisfy the fussiest Brussels bureaucrat.

Indeed the 'downstairs' aspect of Manderston is in some ways even more evocative of the Edwardian age than the 'upstairs'. No detail was too insignificant in the quest for supreme comfort. Even the kitchens were decorated by Kinross, the architect.

The sophistication of the domestic system was such that tradesmen not only had a separate door but a separate corridor. When the bell was rung, the scullery maid could open the door by way of a lever outside the scullery door (which

ABOVE The Kitchen, with sophisticated 'island' cooking range made in Paris by G. Drouet of the Ateliers Briffault.

RIGHT Basement telephone, under sway of the butler.

LEFT The immaculate harness room in the princely Stables: polished rich rosewood, brass and Italian marble.

RIGHT Garden gates built, like everything else at Manderston, on the grand scale.

ABOVE AND BELOW Heraldic adornments on roof (*above*) and gatepiers.

saved her the walk). She would stand at the end of the passage to direct food into whichever of the larders was appropriate. His burden delivered, the trades-man could approach the scullery door – no further – to slake his thirst with a mug of beer from the jar that stood on the table beside it. A place for every-thing, and everything in its place.

In Manderston's heyday, 46 servants (22 inside, 24 out) were required to keep the household ticking over smoothly. Alas, that heyday was all too brief, for Sir James Miller's luck ran out in 1906, when he died, childless, aged 41, only a few months after his dream house was finished.

The baronetcy expired a dozen years later with the death of Sir James's youngest brother, but Sir James's widow lived on at Manderston until the 1930s when the estate was inherited by Major Hugh Bailie (son of Lucky Jim's elder sister, Amy). The Major was a keen horticulturist and after the Second World War planted an extensive and intensely colourful woodland garden with a specialist collection of rhododendrons and azaleas that are a magnificent attraction in their own right.

Before Major Bailie died in 1978 he made over Manderston to his grandson, Adrian Palmer (now the 4th Lord Palmer), elder son of the Major's elder daugh-ter, Lorna, the wife of Col Sir Gordon Palmer. Sir Gordon, who was chairman of the celebrated Reading biscuit firm of Huntley & Palmer (hence the amus-ing exhibition of biscuit tins in the basement), played a significant role in securing Manderston's future by helping to persuade the authorities that the property should be granted Heritage exemption from capital taxation.

Adrian Palmer and his new bride, Cornelia Wadham (sister of the actor Julian Wadham), threw themselves energetically into opening Manderston to the public and making the house pay its way through private and corporate hospitality, film and television location work and all the other necessities of modern country-house life. The Palmers, who have lovingly restored the palatial house and its 56 acres of gardens, represent at its best the practical new generation of historic house owners.

26

ARDKINGLAS

ARGYLL

T HE EDWARDIAN plutocrats were surely dream patrons for architects. At Ardkinglas on Loch Fyne, as at Manderston (*qv*), the building brief was 'nothing but the best and hang the expense'. No wonder the great, if under-valued, architect Robert Lorimer – later Sir Robert and sometimes called 'the Scots Lutyens' – regarded this as his favourite commission. His client Sir Andrew Noble, 1st Bt, the armaments pioneer (and brother-in-law of Isambard Brunel junior), gave him a free hand to design the entire house down to the minutest detail. The only *caveat*, as communicated by Sir Andrew's energetic spinster daughter, Lilias ('Lily'), was to proceed with all haste as the old boy was in his mid-seventies when Lorimer began work in 1906.

Not the least remarkable thing about this lovable, romantic house, which blends so harmoniously with its dramatic Highland landscape, is that it was built merely as a shooting lodge, a holiday home, for Sir Andrew. As chairman of Armstrong's, the armament company, this expatriate Scot was based south of the border, in Northumberland, where he rented such houses as Jesmond Dene (designed by Norman Shaw). Noble was knighted and then, in 1902, created a Baronet in recognition of his important experiments in gunnery and explosives, to which are due the exact science of ballistics and the revolution in composition of gunpowder and the design of guns.

'Shooting lodge' or not, one wonders whether Sir Andrew might have had it in mind to show his old boss, Lord Armstrong, who had commissioned Norman Shaw to turn his modest weekend retreat of Cragside into a cavernous pile, that he too could make something of a splash. Yet, though adorned with Baronial flourishes, Lorimer's deeply sympathetic plan for Ardkinglas harked back to the vernacular architecture of late 17th-century Scotland. The local stone used was a granite of greenish hue patched with gold. The dressed quoins are of a cool, dark cream-coloured stone from Dullatur; the delightfully modelled roofs are covered with Caithness slate now weathered, as Charles Maclean has nicely observed, 'the colour of malt whisky'.

Lorimer envisaged a building that would epitomize, in its pale mass, the rhythms of its setting against the dark, majestic mountains. As such, Ardkinglas can be seen, to quote the architect's biographer, Christopher Hussey, as 'a remarkable instance of expressionist design'. Lorimer's genius was to subordinate the intellectual processes of design to what Hussey calls 'his sensuous intuitions'.

All this aesthetic theorizing was a luxury that could be indulged in later. For the moment, the rush was on to get the house built. Sir Andrew Noble had bought the estate in 1905 from, according to a family memoir, 'the trustees of the estate of two Callander brothers who suffered from intermittent fits of lunacy'. The attraction of the place was that Sir Andrew's Scots–Canadian wife, Margery, was a Campbell and Ardkinglas was very much Campbell country, being across Loch Fyne from Inveraray (*qv*).

In 1396 Sir Colin Campbell, the then *Mac Calein Mor*, granted the estate of Ardkinglas to a younger son, Caileen Oig, 'in all its righteous heaths and marches, or as long as woods shall grow and waters flow'. His descendants had the characteristic Highland history, full of murder, magic, family feuds, witches and warlocks. The 7th Laird was tried thrice for various violent crimes and misdemeanours but escaped conviction, only to drown when his galley capsized. The treacherous 9th Laird had his armorial bearings ceremoniously torn asunder to the sound of trumpets by the Lord Lyon King of Arms at the market cross in Edinburgh in 1662. The 10th Laird, who survived a spell of imprisonment on suspicion of high treason, was created a Baronet in 1679 but this expired with his son, supposedly thanks to a curse laid on him by a speywife.

The old castle at Ardkinglas is recorded as undergoing repairs in 1586. According to an account by Sir John Sinclair (written in 1792, by which time it had

PRECEDING PAGES The Saloon, or Drawing Room, dominated by its massive fireplace, with a lintel carved from a single slab of granite weighing more than five tons.

RIGHT A corner of the Saloon, with its great windows facing Loch Fyne.

ABOVE The building of Ardkinglas was completed in remarkably short order – only 18 months, as the datestone above the front door confirms.

BELOW The entrance front of the lovably Scots creation of Sir Robert Lorimer, which blends so harmoniously with the landscape.

LEFT One of the first country houses to have electricity, Ardkinglas has a series of stylish light fixtures designed by Lorimer to complement his ceilings.

RIGHT The Staircase Hall, with heraldic stained glass.

been razed for over 20 years), it had three separate towers and a stout wall, gatehouse, flanking turrets and a defending tower. The Georgian house that replaced it was already half-derelict by the time Dorothy Wordsworth, the poet's sister, arrived in 1822 to wander through the estate and admire the woods – still one of Ardkinglas's most beautiful features and now boasting some of the finest specimen conifers in Britain, as well as an outstanding collection of rhododendrons.

To enable Ardkinglas Mark III to be built, Lorimer had to arrange the construction of a pier on to Loch Fyne for all the building materials, apart from the local stone for the walls, had to be shipped in from afar. In these circumstances it is all the more remarkable that the new house was actually finished within little more than 18 months.

As Christopher Hussey noted, the impression one takes from Ardkinglas is that 'it is in every way entirely practical, and that the historical flavour of the building has not been won at the cost of any single feature of convenience or modern comfort'. The rooms are grouped under a compact open courtyard. On the ground floor Lorimer furnished Sir Andrew with an oval Study of great charm, and a Smoking-cum-Billiards room. A stately stone staircase leads up to the Morning Room (above the Study) and the house's principal interior, the Saloon, with its windows overlooking Loch Fyne.

This most agreeable oak-panelled room, 45 feet by 22 feet, is dominated by a massive fireplace, which has a lintel carved from a single slab of granite weighing more than five tons. The ceiling is adorned with one of Lorimer's

The tiled kitchen and scullery, still in use.

robust 17th-century-style exercises in garlanded plasterwork. The central panel contains an unexpected painting of Apollo by Roger Fry, the Bloomsbury artist, critic and founder of the Omega Workshop. For all his traditionalist leanings, Lorimer had links with the Arts & Crafts movement and was influenced by Art Nouveau. A close study of the interior of Ardkinglas reveals an enchantingly original series of design details – whether light fixtures, door handles or keyhole flaps.

Fry's painting, however, did not meet with all the Noble family's approval. One opined that it made poor Apollo look as if he was car sick. Sir Humphrey Noble, 4th Bt, Sir Andrew's grandson, tactfully suggested in his evocative memoir *Life in Noble Houses* that 'perhaps one day it will be considered very remarkable'.

Sir Humphrey otherwise considered Ardkinglas a monument to the good taste of his Aunt Lily. This formidable figure was especially insistent that, in accordance with Henry James's description in *The Spoils of Poynton* ('There was not an inch of pasted paper from one end of the great house to the other'), all the rooms at Ardkinglas should be either panelled or covered in white plaster.

The principal bedrooms were also situated on the first floor as well as the Dining Room and the spacious Loggia, looking out to the loch, which is one of Ardkinglas's most enjoyable touches. Most of the bedrooms up on the second floor have pretty plastered and vaulted ceilings. The tower at the top of the house affords glorious views down Loch Fyne to Dunderave and beyond to Inveraray.

The halcyon days of Edwardian sporting holidays at Ardkinglas came to an end in 1915 when Sir Andrew Noble died – 'called over', as a somewhat over-romantic chronicler described it, by the roaring of stags in Glen Kinglas. Subsequently the house ceased to be just a summer retreat; and indeed today it is the centre of a flourishing estate run with commendable gusto and enterprise by John Noble, Sir Andrew's great-grandson.

This refreshingly unstuffy bachelor Laird has ingeniously turned Ardkinglas into a hive of local industry without spoiling its essentially relaxed, comfortable atmosphere. The flagship concern is Loch Fyne Oysters, the now world-famous seafood company which Johnny Noble founded together with Andrew Lane,

Compact hip bath of reassuring depth.

All modern conveniences at Ardkinglas, including this Lorimer-designed shower-cage.

What could be more agreeable? A summer luncheon
laid out in the Loggia.

ABOVE Noble family snapshots.

RIGHT Johnny Noble, the present Laird and visionary seafood champion, at Ardkinglas.

a local fish farmer, in 1978. Their hunch that the clear, unpolluted waters of Loch Fyne, warmed by the Gulf Stream, would prove ideal for growing oysters and other shellfish has been triumphantly vindicated. Today fresh oysters, langoustines, *Bradan Orach* (golden smoked salmon) and other delicacies, not forgetting the legendary Loch Fyne kippers, are sent all over the globe.

Inspired by the tradition of the old 'howfs' (cellars) in 18th-century Edinburgh, where oysters and wine were traditionally enjoyed by all classes, Johnny Noble has also opened a deservedly popular Oyster Bar across the loch from Ardkinglas in a converted farm building at Cairndow, where delicious seafood is served in simple surroundings for one and all to enjoy. Further Loch Fyne Oyster Bars have also been opened in England.

The upshot of all this activity is that, as Johnny Noble points out, the Ardkinglas estate now 'provides as many if not more jobs than it did in Andrew Noble's time'. Life, in short, still goes on in the great houses of Scotland – and there could be no friendlier or more romantic place at which to end our grand tour than Ardkinglas, an amalgam of Scots vernacular architecture through the ages subtly combined with the expansive comfort of *la belle époque*.

Acknowledgements

NO ONE could say – as King George VI is supposed to have sighed to the artist John Piper – that we had trouble with the weather. Throughout the year-long preparation of this book all over Scotland the sun seemed to shine, both literally and metaphorically, on our endeavours. The only clouds that linger in the memory are the unfortunate occasions when the photographer slipped in some woods and fell astride an electric fence ('You know that fence has a current of 4,000 volts,' the owner observed mildly), and when the sturdy old VW Beetle of the author's indefatigable research assistant, Luke Massingberd, came out second-best from a collision with a sheep in the Lammermuir Hills. A few owners of great houses declined to have them included in the book, and one or two Heritage industry *apparatchiks* were less than helpful (and, by a curious coincidence, the houses where they are employed did not happen to make the final cut); but otherwise we received wonderfully generous consideration, co-operation, hospitality and practical advice from owners, administrators, experts, friends and kinfolk.

We would particularly like to thank the following, all of whom made significant contributions to the book and to our enjoyment in producing it: June Marchioness of Aberdeen, Gillon Aitken, the Duke of Argyll, Tony Ashby, the late Duke of Atholl, Mark Bence-Jones, Matthew Benson, Marcus Binney, the Duke and Duchess of Buccleuch, the late Marquess of Bute, Jonathan Cardale, Lt-Col Patrick Cardwell Moore, the late Earl Cawdor and the Dowager Countess Cawdor, Nigel and Henrietta Cayzer, Tim and Jane Clifford, the Earl of Dalkeith, Lady Antonia Dalrymple, Johnny Dumfries, Althea Dundas Bekker, Henrietta Dundas Bekker, Lady Elphinstone, Peter Fairweather, Andrew Fisher, the Knight of Glin, Sir Alistair Grant, Nelly Grant, Robert Gray, the Earl and Countess of Haddington, Christopher Hartley, Sandra Howat, Norman Hudson, James Hunter Blair, Charles Janson, Peter Jervis, Keith Jones, Nina Kapoor, Katie Kerr, Isobel Kyle, David Learmont, Margot Leslie, Michael Leslie, Hamish Leslie Melville, the Marquess of Linlithgow, John McEwen, Angus and Jane Maclay, Sir Charles Maclean, Bt, Gerald and Rosalind Maitland-Carew, the Earl and Countess of Mansfield, Kit Martin, Hannah Mason, Dame Jean Maxwell-Scott, Patricia Maxwell-Scott, Catherine Maxwell Stuart, Flora Maxwell Stuart, Francis and Malinda Menotti, Gian Carlo Menotti, Geoffrey Mitchell, William Mitchell, James Montgomery, Sir David Montgomery, Bt, Caroline Montgomery-Massingberd, John and Marsali Montgomery-Massingberd, the late Sir Iain Moncreiffe of that Ilk, Bt, Teresa Moore, Lord Neidpath, John Noble, Brian Nodes, Paul Normand, Sir Francis Ogilvy, Bt, Lady Ogilvy, Lord and Lady Palmer, Michael Pare, John Powell, Peter Reekie, Peter Reid, Lt-Cdr A.R. Robinson, John Martin Robinson, the Earl and Countess of Rosebery, Michael Sayer, James Scott, David Sharland, Peter Sinclair, Gavin Stamp, Jackie Stewart, Sir Jamie Stormonth Darling, the Earl and Countess of Strathmore, Lord Strathnaver, the Countess of Sutherland, Sir Tatton Sykes, Bt, the Rev Henry Thorold, Hugo and Elizabeth Vickers, Ed Victor, Sir Humphry Wakefield, Bt, the Earl and Countess of Wemyss, and A.N. Wilson.

The photographer would especially like to thank Tony Lawrence at Fuji for the generous donation of film.

Photographic credits are due to the Earl of Dalkeith (for the picture on page 36), the Duke of Buccleuch (page 44), the Dowager Countess Cawdor (page 48) and the Earl of Haddington (both pictures on page 155).

The redoubtable Cynthia Lewis, as ever, typed the manuscript immaculately, battling heroically against the clock. Mary Scott of the publishers was the soul of patience and Alison Wormleighton a sympathetic and painstaking editor. It was a pleasure to collaborate again with the designer, Karen Stafford.

HMM
CSS
London and Kinpurnie, February 1997

– 268 –

Aberdeen, Lord and Lady, *We Twa*, London, 1925
— *More Cracks with We Twa*, London, 1929
Adam, Robert, and James Adam, *The Works in Architecture*, London, 1975 (reprint)
Adam, William, *Vitruvius Scoticus*, Edinburgh, 1980 (reprint)
Apollo magazine: special issue on Dalmeny House, June, 1984
Aslet, Clive, *The Last Country Houses*, New Haven and London, 1982

Bateman, John, *The Great Landowners of Britain and Ireland*, London, 1883 (4th edn)
Beard, Geoffrey, *The Work of Robert Adam*, Edinburgh, 1978
Bence-Jones, Mark, *The Catholic Families*, London, 1992
Bence-Jones, Mark and Hugh Montgomery-Massingberd, *The British Aristocracy*, London, 1979
Billings, R.W., *The Antiquities of Scotland*, Edinburgh, 1852 (4 vols)
Binney, Marcus, 'Gothic Revival', *The Times Magazine*, June 10, 1995
Binney, Marcus, John Harris and Emma Winnington, *Lost Houses of Scotland*, London, 1980
Binney, Marcus, and Kit Martin, *The Country House: To Be Or Not To Be?*, London, 1982
Blair Castle, Derby, 1991
Bolton, Arthur T., *The Architecture of Robert and James Adam*, London, 1922 (2 vols)
Bowhill, Derby, 1981
Burke, Sir Bernard, *Burke's Peerage, Baronetage & Knightage*, London, 1826-1970 (105 editions)
— *Burke's Landed Gentry*, London, 1833-1972 (18 editions)
— *A Visitation of the Seats and Arms of the Noblemen and Gentlemen of Great Britain and Ireland*, London, 1852-5 (4 vols)
— *The Romance of the Aristocracy*, London, 1855 (3 vols)
— *Family Romance*, London, 1860
— *Vicissitudes of Families*, London, 1883 (2 vols)

Burke's Dormant and Extinct Peerages, London, 1969 (reprint)

Campbell, Colen, *Vitruvius Britannicus*, London, 1715-25 (3 vols)
Cantlie, Hugh, *Ancestral Castles of Scotland*, London, 1992
Cawdor, 6th Earl, *Cawdor Castle*, Cawdor, 1992
G.E.C. (okayne), *The Complete Baronetage*, Gloucester, 1983 (reprint, with introduction by Hugh Montgomery-Massingberd)
G.E.C. and others (eds), *The Complete Peerage*, London, 1910-59 (13 vols); Gloucester, 1982 (microprint, 6 vols)
Colvin, H.M., *A Biographical Dictionary of British Architects, 1600-1840*, London, 1978
Connachan-Holmes, John, *Country Houses of Scotland*, Isle of Colonsay, 1995
Cornforth, John, *Country Houses in Britain: Can They Survive?*, London, 1972
— 'Bowhill, Selkirk', *Country Life*, June 5, 12, 19 and 26, 1975
— 'Duff House, Banffshire', *Country Life*, September 21, 1995
— 'The House of Dun, Angus', *Country Life*, November 10, 1986, and June 22, 1989
— 'Manderston, Berwickshire', *Country Life*, February 15 and 22 and March 1, 1979 and August 26, 1993
— 'Newhailes, East Lothian', *Country Life*, November 21 and 28, 1996
— 'Scone Palace, Perthshire', *Country Life*, August 11 and 18, 1988
Country Life: see Binney, Duncan, Girouard, Hall, Hunt, Pryke, Robinson and Rowan
Craik, Sir Henry, *A Century of Scottish History*, London, 1901

Daiches, David, *Sir Walter Scott*, London, 1971
Dictionary of National Biography
Douglas, Sir Robert (ed), *Peerage of Scotland*, Edinburgh, 1813 (2nd edn, 2 vols)
Drumlanrig Castle, Selkirk, 1989
Drummond, Maldwin (ed), *John Bute*, Wilby, 1996

Dunbar, John G., *The Historic Architecture of Scotland*, London, 1996
— *Sir William Bruce, 1630-1710*, Edinburgh, 1970
Duncan, Paul, 'Newhailes, East Lothian', *Country Life*, January 29 and February 5, 1987
Dunrobin Castle, Derby, 1995

Fawcett, Jane (ed), *Seven Victorian Architects*, London, 1976
Fedden, Robin, and John Kenworthy-Browne, *The Country House Guide*, London, 1979 (with Scottish section by Colin McWilliam)
Fenwick, Hubert, *Architect Royal: The Life and Works of Sir William Bruce*, London, 1970
— *Scotland's Castles*, London, 1976
— *Scotland's Historic Buildings*, London, 1974
— *Scottish Baronial Houses*, London, 1986
Fleming, John, *Scottish Country Houses and Gardens Open to the Public*, London, 1954
Forman, Sheila, *Scottish Country Houses and Castles*, Glasgow, 1967

Gifford, John, *The Buildings of Scotland: Highlands and Islands*, London, 1992
— *The Buildings of Scotland: Dumfries and Galloway*, London, 1996
Girouard, Mark, *Historic Houses of Britain*, London, 1979
— *The Victorian Country House*, New Haven and London, 1979
— 'Kinross House, Kinross-shire', *Country Life*, March 25 and April 1, 1965
Gordon, Archie, *A Wild Flight of Gordons*
Gordon, Sir Robert, *A Genealogical History of the Earldom of Sutherland*, Edinburgh, 1813
Gow, Ian, and Timothy Clifford, *Duff House*, Edinburgh, 1995
Greville, Charles, *Journals of the Reign of Queen Victoria, 1837-1952*, London, 1885 (3 vols)
Grierson, Sir H.J.C. (ed), *Letters of Sir Walter Scott*, London 1932-7 (12 vols)

Hall, Michael, 'Mount Stuart, Isle of Bute', *Country Life*, June 15, 1995

Hartley, Christopher, *Haddo House*, Edinburgh, 1989

— *The House of Dun*, Edinburgh, 1992

Hill, Oliver, *Scottish Castles of the 16th and 17th Centuries*, London, 1953

Hopetoun House, Derby, 1996

Hunt, John, 'Gosford, East Lothian', *Country Life*, October 21 and November 4, 1971

Hussey, Christopher, *The Work of Sir Robert Lorimer*, London, 1931

Innes-Smith, R., *Glamis Castle*, Derby, 1993

Jackson-Stops, Gervase (ed), *Treasure Houses of Britain*, New Haven and London, 1985

Johnson, Edgar, *Sir Walter Scott: The Great Unknown*, London, 1970

Learmont, David, and Gordon Riddle, *Culzean Castle and Country Park*, Edinburgh, 1992

Lees-Milne, James, *The Age of Adam*, London, 1947

Lindsay, Ian G., and Mary Cosh, *Inveraray and the Dukes of Argyll*, Edinburgh, 1973

Lockhart, John Gibson, *Life of Scott*, Edinburgh, 1837-8

Macaulay, James, *The Classical Country House in Scotland, 1660-1800*, London, 1987

— *The Gothic Revival, 1745-1845*, Glasgow and London, 1975

Macaulay, T.B., *History of England*, London, 1849-61 (5 vols)

MacGibbon, David, and Thomas Ross, *The Castellated and Domestic Architecture of Scotland*, Edinburgh, 1887-92 (5 vols)

Macky, John, *Journey through Scotland*, Edinburgh, 1723

Maclean, Charles, and Christopher Simon Sykes, *Scottish Country*, London, 1992

Maclean, Fitzroy, *A Concise History of Scotland*, London, 1970

McWilliam, Colin, *The Buildings of Scotland: Lothian*, London, 1978

Magnusson, Magnus, *Treasures of Scotland*, London, 1981

Manderston, Wardington

Markham, Sarah, *John Loveday of Caversham, 1711-89*, Wilton, 1984

Masters, Brian, *The Dukes*, London, 1980 (2nd edn)

Maxwell-Scott, Maj-Gen Sir Walter, Bt, *Abbotsford*, Abbotsford

Maxwell Stuart, Flora, *Lady Nithsdale and the Jacobites*, Traquair, 1995

Mellerstain, Derby, 1988

Moncreiffe of that Ilk, Sir Iain, Bt, *The Highland Clans*, London, 1982 (2nd edn)

Montgomery-Massingberd, Hugh, *Great British Families*, London and Exeter, 1988

— 'Heritage' (and 'Family Seats') articles in *The Field*, 1976-1987, and *The Daily Telegraph*, 1987-96

Montgomery-Massingberd, Hugh (ed), *Lord of the Dance: A Moncreiffe Miscellany*, London, 1986

Mount, Ferdinand, *Umbrella*, London, 1994

Neale, J.P., *Views of the Seats of Noblemen and Gentlemen*, London, 1819.

Nicolson, Nigel, *Great Houses of Britain*, London, 1978

Noble, Sir Humphrey, Bt, *Life in Noble Houses*, 1969

Pattullo, Nan, *Castles, Houses and Gardens of Scotland*, Edinburgh, 1967

Petzsch, Helmut, *Architecture in Scotland*, London, 1971

Prentice, Robin (ed), *The National Trust for Scotland Guide*, London, 1981 (3rd edn)

Pryke, Sebastian, 'Hopetoun House, West Lothian', *Country Life*, August 10, 1995

Richardson, Sir Albert, *Robert Mylne, Architect and Engineer, 1782-1811*, London, 1955

Robinson, John Martin, *The Latest Country Houses*, London, 1984

— 'Dalmeny House, West Lothian', *Country Life*, August 17 and 24, 1989

Rosebery, Countess of, *Dalmeny House*, Dalmeny

Rowan, Alistair, 'Yester House, East Lothian', *Country Life*, August 5, 16 and 23, 1973

Rykwert, Joseph, and Anne Rykwert, *The Brothers Adam*, London, 1985

Sayer, Michael, and Hugh Massingberd, *The Disintegration of a Heritage: Country Houses and their Collections*, Wilby, 1993

Savage, Peter, *Lorimer and the Edinburgh Craft Designers*, Edinburgh, 1980

Scone Palace, Scone

Scott, Walter, *Lay of the Last Minstrel*, Edinburgh, 1805

Shakespeare, William, *Macbeth*, 1606 (?)

Sitwell, Sacheverell, *British Architects and Craftsmen*, London, 1945

Small, *Castles and Mansions of the Lothians*, Edinburgh, 1883

Smout, T.C., *History of the Scottish People 1560-1830*, London, 1969

Stamp, Gavin, *Robert Weir Schultz, Architect, and His Work for the Marquess of Bute*, London, 1981

Stamp, Gavin (ed), *Mount Stuart House and Gardens*, Mount Stuart, 1995

Stewart, A.F. (ed), *Horace Walpole: Last Journals*, London, 1910

Stewart, J.L.M., *The Story of the Atholl Highlanders*, Blair Atholl, 1987

Stirling Maxwell, Sir John, Bt, *Scottish Homes and Shrines*, London, 1938

Stormonth Darling, Sir Jamie, and Robin Prentice, *Culzean: The Continuing Challenge*, Edinburgh, 1985

Strong, Roy, Marcus Binney, John Harris *et al*, *The Destruction of the Country House*, London, 1974

Stuart, Denis, *Dear Duchess: Millicent Duchess of Sutherland 1867-1955*, London, 1982

Sutherland, Douglas, *The Landowners*, London, 1968

Sykes, Christopher Simon, *Black Sheep*, London, 1982

Tait, A.A., *Duff House*, Edinburgh, 1985

— *Treasures in Trust*, Edinburgh, 1981

Tait, J.G. (ed), *Sir Walter Scott's Journal*, Edinburgh, 1939-46 (3 vols)

Thirlestane Castle, Wardington

Traquair, Traquair, 1992

Vickers, Hugo, *The Kiss*, London, 1996

Walker, N.H., *Kinross House*, 1990

Walpole, Horace, *Letters*, Oxford 1903-8 and 1918-25, London, 1937-

— *Memories of the Reign of King George III*, London, 1894 (4 vols)

Wilson, A.N., *The Laird of Abbotsford*, Oxford, 1980

Yarwood, Doreen, *Robert Adam*, London, 1970